A LEXICON OF ORAL ADVOCACY

Frank M. Coffin

NITA

Library of Congress Catalog Card Number: 84-62201

PRINTED IN THE UNITED STATES OF AMERICA

Copies of this book are available upon request from the National Institute for Trial Advocacy. Please direct inquiries to:

National Institute for Trial Advocacy
Administrator's Office
1507 Energy Park Drive
St. Paul, Minnesota 55108
(612) 644-0323

By Frank M. Coffin

Witness for AID
(1964)

The Ways of a Judge:
Reflections from the Federal Appellate Bench
(1980)

TABLE OF CONTENTS

So to describe this word is vastly to underestimate its complexity. Complexity is inherent, since candor describes a spokesman who always labors in a tension between duty to client and duty to court.

CHESHIRE CAT **31**

The lawyer who so completely shares with the judges their vast knowledge of the law that he feels no compulsion to explain either the facts or the law, preferring to smile instead.

CHUTZPAH **32**

The quality of testing judges' willingness to suspend their disbelief. It is gall carried to a point of magnificent supererogation. (But, like almost any other vice, it has its place.)

CLIENT IN COURT **33**

A device which, when calculated to generate sympathy, more often than not backfires.

CONFIDENCE **35**

A quality which, however manifested by counsel, if it stems from hard analysis, stands a good chance of spreading its benign influence to the court.

CONTROL (and its loss) **39**

The ability to give some direction to the discussion of issues. This could be subtitled control of time, of self, of court, or of argument.

CREDIBILITY (a misplaced argument) **48**

This is an argument that the testimony of a key witness is so unbelievable that the verdict or judgment below must be reversed. While an obviously proper argument to make to the finder of fact, it is almost never justified at the appellate level.

DANCER **50**

An advocate who believes that he can infuse strength into an otherwise flaccid case by substituting body dynamics for the spoken word.

chronic suicidal complex, throws caution and diplomacy to the winds, draws his sword and takes on all judges at once.

HARE 67

An advocate who is well prepared and assumes that the court is as thoroughly conversant with all of the facts and law as he is. He therefore tries to cover as much ground as possible by (a) talking very rapidly, (b) making great leaps from issue to issue, or (c) doing both.

HOUSE COUNSEL (away from home) 68

A lawyer who serves as the permanent "inside" legal adviser to a corporation. Because of the high fees charged by the major law firms, many corporations are said to be utilizing house counsel more and more. But it is a rare "inside" adviser who is also a good "outside" advocate.

JUDGES 69

Lawyers who were once advocates, whose job now is to decide among advocates, and who, in the process of deciding, will advocate their positions to their colleagues. Judges have the power to make oral presentations a shambles or a stimulating aid to expeditious and sound decisions.

JURY LAWYER (without a jury) 74

A lawyer who makes the mistake of thinking that three or more appellate judges sitting behind a bench respond to the same approaches as do six to twelve jurors sitting in a jury box.

LISTENING 76

A rare quality in an advocate that, when a judge asks him a question, causes him to suspend his own thinking, concentrate on what the judge is saying, and try to see what bothers him.

MARSHALLING 79

The finale and capstone of an effective oral presentation in which the advocate brings together in succinct, highlighted form all of the facts

PREFACE

This slim volume makes no claim to developing a set of principles and precepts. It does aspire to give the reader a base on which to build his or her own conduct as an oral advocate.

Like most people who think about oral advocacy, I regard it as more art than science or trade. So thinking, I have tried to emulate the visual artist who, rather than study texts and listen to lectures, supplements his own studio efforts with observing and analyzing others' productions, visiting museums, seeing what works and what doesn't.

My device for approximating such an approach is the following Lexicon in which I have tried to describe familiar types of advocates and advocacy. Most of what I have written began in rough notes that I made over a period of years at the time of each oral argument in our court. My jottings would try to capture a few impressions. Shortly after the argument I would write a more expanded version. Ultimately I organized my notes in categories and winnowed out the duplications and other chaff. What remains represents the distillations from some four to five hundred arguments by lawyers on appeal. I have not felt bound by the lexicon format; some letters of the alphabet have several entries while others have none.

My method is not too different from that of Dr. Johnson who concocted his famous Dictionary by using a wealth of apt quotations to illustrate the nuances of words. Just as he said in his Preface that he "extracted from philosophers principles of science; . . . from divines striking exhortations; and from poets beautiful description,"[1] I can say that I have extracted from lawyers – and judges – the effective and the maladroit, the banal and the exquisite. My hope is that these extracts will help the practitioner identify both strengths to cultivate and weaknesses to avoid – and thus help all of us . . . self, client, and us captive audiences, the appellate judges.

There is one other way of capturing the idiosyncrasies of lawyers than the verbal. It is the graphic way as Daumier so eloquently demonstrated. My Daumier is my son Douglas to whom I am indebted for both the design and the illustrations of this work. That the National Institute of Trial Advocacy was willing to embark on such a venture as this is evidence enough of its flexibility, boldness, and, I pray, sound judgment.

FMC

South Portland
Maine

---

[1]W. Jackson Bate, Samuel Johnson. N.Y. and London: Harcourt Brace Jovanovich, 1975 and 1977; p. 250.

INTRODUCTORY NOTE

The Limits and Possibilities of Contemporary Advocacy

Just as children used to attend dancing school to learn dance steps which they would seldom have occasion to use in later years, and just as the nations of the world have often trained their military forces and perfected their fortifications to deal with the strategies of past, but not future, wars, so the literature and lore of oral advocacy and even the moot courts of the law schools fall far short of addressing the contemporary conditions of presenting a case to an appellate court.

Some schools put their students through paces reminiscent of the elegantly formal and leisurely style of the nineteenth century, when a Daniel Webster could address the Supreme Court for hours and even days in convoluted, orotund prose, with little danger of interruption from the bench. Although no such oratorical marathons are perpetrated today, it is not unusual for one law student on a moot court team to be expected to narrate the facts for ten minutes and each of two others to speak for a half hour on a preassigned and preannounced set of issues. The emphasis on mere narration, the allocation of issues between different advocates, and the liberal allowance of time – over an hour per side – replicate no conditions in real life that I have seen.

The past few decades have seen a subtle but fundamental change in what we might call the dimensions of appellate advocacy. One dimension, time, has experienced a dramatic foreshortening: the old custom of an hour per side first dwindled to a half hour and now in perhaps a majority of cases to fifteen or twenty minutes, with 10 minute periods being assigned with increasing frequency. The pressures on time have radically changed two other dimensions, formality and the nature of the participation by the bench. Precisely because time has been so sharply telescoped, judges cannot expect to learn everything they would need to know by sitting back and listening. If they are bothered about something, they had better bring the matter up before time runs out. This means that an advocate cannot safely expect to be able to complete a nicely prepared set of formal remarks. And it also means that appellate benches are no longer passive but active. Indeed, although I have not seen the metamorphosis so described, the nature of appellate argument has undergone a major systemic change – from a purely adversarial system to one closely approaching the civil law's inquisitorial system, with judges not only participating but often dominating the oral proceeding.

As a result of these changes, I think it unrealistic to continue to think of oral advocacy exclusively in terms of the phrase "oral argument." The processes of logical reasoning, though indispensable in appellate advocacy, are but one of a number of sub-sets of the modes of oral interchange with an active bench. Just as tragedy is only one form of drama, which encompasses all modes of acting before an audience, so argument is only one way in which lawyers use the short time when they stand at a lectern and have the undivided attention of an appellate bench.

It is time for both the law schools and would-be appellate advocates to recognize the wide spectrum of uses which the present-day confrontation between judges and advocates serves. As each appellate occasion is seen to focus on a particular use, the role of the advocate changes together with what is appropriate in style and content of presentation.

Here is my own attempt to identify the uses of today's appellate presentations:

Traditional Argument. Marshalling evidence to support verdicts, citing and distinguishing legal precedents, interpreting statutes, making arguments from logic, policy, and history.

General Presentation of Facts. Sometimes the major, if not the only, purpose that should be served by an oral presentation is making clear what the relevant facts are. The complex devices involved in some product liability cases or the tortuous stories of criminal conspiracies need effective oral exposition and narration. If an advocate fills this need, he should feel that he has done all he could under the circumstances to help the court and his client.

Correcting or Confirming Understanding. Judges who have read briefs in advance have a general idea of the case, but their preparation is usually hasty. They will often miss or fail to appreciate fully a fact, a procedural point, a legal authority, or even the nature of the issue before the court. Once a judge asks a question explicitly indicating his ignorance or uncertainty, counsel can quickly remedy any defect of understanding. Often a judge may not know that he has a misperception; in such a case counsel's ear must be attuned to an unarticulated misunderstanding. Sometimes the fault is entirely counsel's: the briefs may be so poorly done that the only chance for enlightenment is through the oral presentation. The judge's question or comment may not be at all important in itself; but effective handling of the concern may, as one practitioner emphasized to me, make the difference between winning and losing.

Finally, if counsel's case is strong and his brief is a good one, judges may show by their questions that all they need is rather succinct confirmation; lengthy and detailed exegesis will weaken rather than strengthen their impression. In all these situations the role of counsel is to supply the court's directly expressed or indirectly exhibited need for specific information. The best "argument" may be a few brief factual statements.

Exploration of Remedy. Not infrequently briefs may address the merits and demerits of a case exhaustively, with little or no attention to the nature and scope of a remedy if a party is held to prevail on the merits. The confrontation of judges and lawyers in such a case may be most fruitfully exploited to determine whether a remand to the trial court is necessary, whether an injunction is called for or only a declaratory judgment, what the scope of any injunction should be, whether any further hearings should be held and if so what should be their nature, etc. Even if an advocate fervently hopes that the court will not have to face these questions, he is well advised to have given thought to them so that his responses will be well considered. These may be the most salient part of his advocacy.

Mootness or Prematurity. Every once in a while, often enough to cause concern, a case reaches the appellate court either *before* it should reach it or *after* it has ceased to be a case. When questions from the bench elicit such an embarrassing situation, I know of nothing for counsel to do except concede in as good grace as possible . . . and sit down. In case of doubt counsel should ask leave to submit a supplemental memorandum.

Examining Impact of Recent Cases. Between the time when the trial court or agency imposed its judgment and the presentation of the appeal, the Supreme Court or other courts may have issued an important opinion that touches upon the case. The most important function of the oral presentation under these circumstances may simply be a full and candid discussion of why the new case does or does not affect the issues on appeal. I quickly add that the advocate should not await oral argument to discuss such a case. He should promptly file a supplemental memorandum to reveal and briefly analyze it.

Judges' Education of Their Colleagues. If a judge has thought long and hard about a case and has developed some unusual views, he will want to try them out not only on the advocates but on his fellow judges. This happens most commonly when a judge senses that an apparently easy affirmance has some concealed problems of considerable difficulty. For example, an appellant whose case looks almost frivolous may have hit upon a winning issue even though it is hidden in a poor brief among a dozen losing issues. In such a case the judge's questions are not merely testing counsel but signalling to the other judges that the case is far more interesting than it first appeared. A keen observer at court would take note of the subtle signs of quickening interest – judges leaning forward, making notes, listening intently, perhaps even glancing at a colleague. In all probability the advocate who receives this kind of support from a judge is not a very good one, or he would have put his own best foot forward. By the same token the advocate whose case may be adversely affected by the judge's queries would, if he had prepared thoroughly, usually have discovered the same issue that the judge did and would be able to deal with it. Advocates, however, like judges, are human and occasionally may overlook an important issue. If this happens, about the best one can do is ask for a few days to respond to the issue unearthed by the judge.

Provision of a Public Forum. What tends to be overlooked in discussing the uses of appellate argument is the dual function of public access and the enhancement of public understanding. An important part of the decision process is open to the press, the public, and to the parties themselves. To the extent that both the advocates and the judges have invested effort in preparation to make the oral presentation and colloquy as useful as possible will respect for the process be engendered.

The simplistic view that argument is the only activity performed by lawyers in appearing before a bench of appellate judges is linked with the equally unreal idea that the only goal of the advocate is to win. The unspoken syllogism is:

Judges are persuaded by the cleverest argument.
By dint of hard work and/or sheer brilliance one lawyer will be cleverer than his opponent.
Therefore, such a lawyer will win.

Such a proposition, when so baldly spelled out, is preposterous. But one suspects that something like it underlies the expectations of far too many would-be advocates, and perhaps most clients.

Yet what is left if this illusion of victory going to the swift and clever is demolished? If judges are expected to penetrate beneath every misleading facade and reach the underlying facts and relevant law and correct result, of what importance is excellence in appellate advocacy? Moreover, if victory is not the reliable measure of excellence, in what does excellence consist? It seems to me that a lawyer best serves his client and his own self-esteem if he sees clearly in any given case the realistic ends to be served by his personal appearance before an appellate bench. Without any pretension of exhausting the possibilities, I set forth the following types of situations in which counsel can exercise an influence.

An effective oral presentation, filling the particular needs of the judges, contributes mightily to the speed and quality of the court's decision.

In a small minority of cases where law or facts or policies are evenly balanced, a superior presentation can in itself account for victory.

A good oral advocate can compensate for a poor brief which he or an associate may have written long ago in too much haste.

An effective oral presentation is good insurance against losing a deserving case.

Since judges are fallible, an effective oral presentation can even bring the advocate an undeserved victory.

As we have noted, a well-prepared advocate can correct otherwise fatal misperceptions by judges.

If a judge floats some new arguments, introduces new issues, or exhibits some particular concerns, counsel can deal with them. The advocate may concede non-crucial points, distinguish troublesome cases, acknowledge that his argument need not be carried to its logical extent and agree that relief may be limited to avoid the prospect of opening a floodgate.

Counsel often can affect the tone, tenor, and scope of an opinion, e.g., by achieving a broad precedent or a unanimous court in winning or by obtaining a narrow holding or a strong dissent in losing.

Similarly, counsel can be instrumental in helping shape a remedy.

Counsel can derive the professional satisfaction of having helped in guiding the court in contributing to the sound development of the law.

ACTOR

An advocate who views oral argument as an exclusively theatrical occasion.

Because good theater seeks usually to touch the emotions, while argument appeals to the intellect, it is not surprising that seldom do these twain agreeably meet. The actor is not the same role model as the jury lawyer, *see infra*. The latter's histrionics are selected and shaped for a particular audience, the jury. The actor/advocate observes no such limitation. For him all the world's a stage, including the normally hushed and cerebral appellate courtroom.

One of my most predictable of thespians stimulated this entry in my notes:

"A familiar figure and a flamboyant one. He is always to be

counted on for a colorful and unhelpful performance. He struts back and forth behind the lectern, promenading like a peacock, swiveling to glimpse the audience behind him, speaking in stentorian tones, gesticulating vigorously if somewhat randomly. I used to try to domesticate this flamboyant fowl, but now I know better. My problem is that he is never quite vulnerable to a lethal blow. He is never too far off base and in a queer way makes points that cannot readily be dismissed. So I resign myself to his performance, knowing he'll take me for another wild ride."

Just to illustrate the proposition that in advocacy there are few things that one can say should never be done, I include an instance of effective acting. A youngish but experienced trial and appellate lawyer was attacking a jury instruction given in the trial court. With wrinkled brow and painfully serious demeanor he recreated the atmosphere of the trial and made us sense how the instruction had sounded to the jury. He stopped short of being "theatrical." I thought what he did was an appropriate way of breathing life into the cold transcript.

AD HOMINEM

A remark, having nothing to do with the law or facts of a case but most often with the niceness or naughtiness of a party or a counsel, calculated to make points with the judge. Literal meaning: ***"to the man" but more accurately "for the birds."***

Here are a few garden varieties. An attorney in his forties, arguing just after one of my colleagues had joined our court: "This is my first case before a new judge." As I tried to fathom the relevance of this intelligence, the attorney followed up with, "My client is in the first row."

A solo practitioner in his late thirties begins, "This is the first time in my 17 years of practice that I've come across the river to argue a case here." His performance proved that he was telling the truth.

Anxious appellant counsel are not the only offenders. An assistant United States Attorney, arguing in support of a conviction, began, inauspiciously, by asking a judge to repeat a question, then replied, "I'm drawing a blank. I'll pass on to the other points and perhaps the answer will occur to me." Then we had to ask him why we should consider three issues he had not argued to the trial court. Finally, perhaps in desperation, he unveiled his clinching argument against giving defendant a new trial: "As the Chief Justice has said, there must be an end some time to court proceedings. Why," he added, waving a newspaper clipping, "this appellant says that if he wins this case, he'll become a lawyer."

Arrogance

An inescapable odor permeating the argument of the lawyer who senses the superiority of his own mind to the more modest attainments of the judges. Synonyms: ***condescension, impatience, patronizing.*** See also ***"Unctuousness,"*** infra.

Arrogance in advocacy as elsewhere in life wears many disguises. Sometimes, though rarely, it is undisguised. A lawyer will occasionally be so infuriated at being enmeshed in hideously protracted litigation, so angry with his adversary counsel or the opposing party, or so skeptical of the court's ability to act responsibly that his strident tone of voice, haughty bearing, apoplectic look, and choice of language bespeak arrogance in the clearest of terms. On such occasions the lawyer (who has of course ceased being much of an advocate . . . except for the other side) may deign to let the court know how many cases in this precise field he has tried and how often eminent judges have held in his favor.

Sometimes arrogance lies in a look. I interrupt a senior partner from a big firm, an expert in his field. He looks at me incredulously, pityingly. On another occasion, counsel is obviously completely at home in court (perhaps feeling more at home than we do); with hands in his pockets, he swivels from side to side and shares his perceptions with his equals behind the bench. So long as he is allowed to pursue his thought, all is well. But if a judge exhibits a slowness to comprehend, counsel raises

his voice and looks at his watch to convey the message that time's a-wasting.

Arrogance is bad, not because it is unmannerly, but because it tempts judges to be unjudicial. It stimulates a devilish – or is it merely human? – desire to rule against the party because of the lawyer's communicated sense of superiority.

I don't wish to fault counsel too much. A good lawyer will have dug far deeper into his case than the judge. Quite often the questions from the bench will be repetitive, irrelevant, unnecessary, or even obtuse. Dealing with these without conveying an impression (whether truly felt or not) of arrogance is not easy.

Ignoring a question as not worthy of attention is the worst approach. A crisp, over-succinct brush-off answer is hardly better, as is the response that begins, "As I said before . . ." or "Let me repeat . . . " Nor does it help to be over-didactic and adopt a "back-to-the-drawing-board" tone appropriate for the lower elementary grades.

The antidote for arrogance or its appearance may require an act of will: forcefully saying to oneself, "Now remember, these judges are trying. They have dozens of other cases on their minds. Try to put yourself in their place." With luck counsel might then reply to a less than astute question thusly: "I'm sorry, Your Honor. I've been so close to this case that I may take too many things for granted. What I meant to convey was this . . . ."

BACKBENCHER

An advocate whose remarks at the lectern are the least important part of his argument. His preferred locus is at the counsel table; his preferred time is when his adversary is addressing the court; and his preferred languages are body English and pantomimicry.

He is most dangerous before (or after) he addresses the court. His gamut includes:

The Violently Confirming Nod (after a judge asks his adversary a question) meaning "That's precisely right, Your Honor.

You've hit the nail right on the head."

The Emphatic Shake (after a statement by his adversary at the lectern) meaning "Your Honors, that's what *he* says but that isn't the way it happened."

The Look of Scorn meaning "This lawyer is to be pitied; his client is such a contemptible liar."

The Home Free Look (after an exchange between his adversary and a judge) meaning "Well done, Your Honor. You've certainly seen through his case."

Seismic Shock (after a particularly telling argument of his adversary) meaning "Incredible that he could stoop so low." This response can range from lifting one brow skeptically, lifting both brows, opening wide the mouth, lifting both hands palms up, to turning to the rear of the courtroom and waving a clenched fist for the benefit of his client.

How do judges deal with this character? Some are so wrapped up in their questioning of the front bencher at the lectern that they are unaware of the extra argument going on. Some pretend not to notice. If the lawyer is young or new to the court, a judge will gently interrupt the argument and address the offender thusly, "Counsel, we know you have much to say but your turn will come" or "Counsel, you've had your say; give your brother his." But if the lawyer should know better, a judge is likely to observe that he should subside and that if he cannot contain himself, he should withdraw. Either approach, soft or hard, is not a pleasant experience for counsel . . . particularly if his client is present.

BORE (monumental)

To be distinguished from "small bore," an advocate who is merely dull and tedious.

The monumental bore is more of a problem for a court. His flatulence, bumbling, and wandering are so outrageous that a judge cannot resist wading in with what he thinks is trenchant criticism. In fact, the judge, infuriated by counsel's maddening blandness, winds up making an imprudent comment. This is precisely what the bore, at heart a sly old fox, wishes. With injured innocence, he then shows the judge how unfair his comment was. This leaves the judge shaking with the palsy of impotent fury, from which state he does not emerge for the remainder of the argument. Counsel may not be an intentional judge-baiter, but his natural endowments eminently qualify him for the role.

Here are two enduring memories from my notes:

> "Appellant's counsel was a somewhat sleazy old fox who had long irked me with his generally frivolous appeals. I came to argument, ready, in a small way, for blood. Appellant's major issue was the correctness of a jury instruction. I had noticed, however, that he never objected to the charge at trial. This fact was conveniently omitted from the brief. Now, thought I, I could nail him for misleading the court. But when I suggested that he had misled us by not revealing that no objection had been made, he pointed to one small sentence at the end of the brief where he concluded by saying that the charge constituted 'plain error,' therefore implying that this is the kind of error that one can complain of even though no objection was made at trial. So I could not quite accuse him of misleading."

> "Appellant's counsel had on more occasions than I care to remember exhibited his talent for exacerbation. He had submitted a brief that not only was excessive in length but that consisted mostly of overheated and irrelevant rhetoric, and facts that were not of record. I read each extravagant page, my gorge rising. Finally, I thought, this particular bore would receive his comeuppance. But just a few pages from the end I found an argument hidden away to which I had no answer. We had to swallow hard and grant him a remand, as he requested, to the trial court. Once again a monumental bore made us eat crow."

Candor

One of the most prized attributes of a good advocate, this virtue is usually described in absolute terms; i.e., either a lawyer is candid or he is not; or, candor requires one to level completely with the court. So to describe the word is vastly to underestimate its complexity. Complexity is inherent, since candor describes a spokesman who always labors in a tension between duty to client and duty to court.

Zero percent candor is easy to spot . . . the advocate who omits some telling fact from his account of a case, who fails to mention a key precedent, who neglects to say that his own principal case authority has been overruled, who challenges evidentiary rulings or objections at a trial without telling the court that no objection had been noted.

One hundred percent candor is, from the client's point of view, just as lethal. "I am court-appointed counsel" can often be translated as "I am just doing my job. I didn't choose this client or case." "I wasn't trial counsel below" converts into "Someone else made a botch of this; I haven't got much to work with on appeal." One might as well confide to the court, "I tried to argue my client out of appeal, but he insisted."

The precise amount of candor that gives maximum assistance to the court without invading any legitimate interest of the client is something that only the most sensitive advocate can work out in a specific case. When this happens, the impression given is one of admirable grace. Like most things giving this impression, candor is most reliably achieved with the assistance of forethought. The discipline of preparation for oral argument should include a conscious inventory of facts, inferences, arguments, and issues which counsel *can* fairly concede without jeopardizing his client – and those which counsel *should* take the initiative in conceding.

Frequently the problem of striking this balance results from a question by one of the judges. A tough and probably unfair question is: "Counsel, what do you consider your most important issue?" A lawyer is tempted to waffle and say that all are important or else to succumb and identify one issue, at the cost of diminishing all the others. I noted one exchange where counsel was rather magnificent, naming three issues without denigrating others. For example, one omitted issue was whether there was enough evidence of defendant's flight from the arms of the law to justify an instruction that this could be regarded as evidence of guilt. Counsel nicely said, "We could argue all day as to whether the evidence supports the instruction. I'll leave this to my brief."

Occasionally the questions from the bench are simplistic, even obtuse. A judge, temporarily outraged by one side or empathizing with the other, may ask the ultimate question on appeal, only superficially disguised as a hypothetical question: "Don't you concede, counsel, that . . . .?" If the question is of this nature, the advocate should tactfully but candidly expose it for what it is, saying, "Well, Your Honor, that is really the precise issue involved in this appeal. I would make the same argument that I am now making." Perhaps the asking judge will momentarily be miffed that he didn't make more mileage with his question, but the other judges will be relieved that time was not wasted in going around in circles.

There are other times when candor should lead the advocate to make concessions. One such occasion would arise when the advocate is asked to distinguish a case. If it can be clearly and strongly distinguished, well and good; but if it can be distinguished only by resorting to minuscule points of difference, it makes better sense to acknowledge that the case *is* authority for the other side, although wrongly decided. Yet even this can be overdone. I have seen an appellee's counsel go so far overboard in acknowledging the thrust of an adverse decision that her whole case was fatally weakened.

Another occasion calling for a concession would arise if a judge asks if the court could affirm on an issue that the trial judge did not purport to resolve. It is tempting for a lawyer to try to sew up his case without further ado, but a candid acknowledgement that a remand may be necessary may gain credibility far more than straining for a short cut to victory. It is always well for counsel to bear in mind that untenable positions will almost always be exposed as the battalion of three or more judges and their law clerks go to work on the case.

In a sense candor usually involves only the conceding of something most likely to be discovered ultimately. Sometimes, however, there may be a case or fact unlikely to be discovered, which the court is entitled to know; revealing it is candor in its purest form. Yet counsel should not confuse this situation with revealing information that the court is *not* entitled to know. For example, should a judge ask for facts outside the record, which occurred before, during or since trial, counsel should not hesitate to say simply that the record is silent. This advice should work both ways – both when the extra-record facts put one's client in an unfavorable light and when they show the client wreathed in a halo. (In the latter case counsel may be forgiven if he answers a judge, "I wish I could properly reveal the answer to Your Honor, but since it is not of record I cannot.")

Candor toward the court is best viewed as the product of candor toward one's own case. That is, only after one has forced oneself to view one's cause as unsympathetically as others could reasonably view it, does one see the full extent of procedural problems, factual weaknesses, questionable policy implications, and adverse precedents that one must contend with. Having taken this step, counsel is then in a position to place his entire presentation to the court on the bedrock of candor.

Because lawyers ordinarily do not choose their clients for their decency, it happens that they may occasionally represent hard, impersonal, even ruthless bargainers seeking to retain an unfair advantage. Counsel should spend little time in trying to paint a weed as a lily, except to say what can be said positively concerning his client's motives or tactics. Here one is often aided by the fact that fault or human inadequacy is not concentrated solely on one side of a case. Apart from any essential character salvage, counsel might just as well stick to the theme: "Your Honors may very well not have acted as plaintiff did here, but I submit that the question before you is simply whether the words of the statute (or the contract) mean what they say." My notes of one such argument read, "Counsel was cool, dispassionate, conceded injustice, but quietly and unanswerably concluded, 'But that's what the words say.'"

A most unenviable predicament confronts a lawyer with case authority against him – from the very court to which he has carried his appeal. Indeed, in a civil case a lawyer or his client, or both, face the danger of having to pay double costs or attorney's fees for the other side as a sanction for bringing a frivolous appeal. In a criminal case a court is not likely so to sanction a defendant's lawyer but the threshold obstacle remains to be dealt with. One lawyer I recall had a miserable case but marvelous sangfroid. He was challenging a trial court's instructions of "reasonable doubt," which were similar to those we had criticized on numerous occasions, never quite deeming them such errors as to justify reversal of a conviction. Here is the colloquy:

Judge (a visitor to our court): "I have read three opinions of this court reviewing this precise charge, but none of them led to a reversal."

Counsel: "I concede I have two strikes against me. But after these three criticizing opinions, I submit that the time has come for this court to reverse."

He could have added, "if it wishes to retain its credibility among trial judges." He refrained, but his argument was a powerful one. If it didn't prevail in that case, it might very well in the next.

A successful example of this approach occurred in a maritime accident case where counsel faced not only adverse authority squarely on point from our court but *recent* such authority. He began by stating that he fully understood his burden in trying to persuade us that we wrongly decided our recent case. But we should undo our error as quickly as possible. And we did!

CHESHIRE CAT

The lawyer who so completely shares with the judges their vast knowledge of the law that he feels no compulsion to explain either the facts or the law, preferring to smile instead.

His chosen instrument of advocacy is a broad, confident, fixed smile. This seems to cloak, for him if for no one else, the fact that he has a difficult, uphill road to travel. He says a few words, then beams at the court as if to say, "You and I alone understand this case. There is no point in my telling you what we both already know."

Just as Alice in Wonderland, we continue to see the grin long after the advocate has vanished from view . . . a process that begins when he approaches the lectern.

CHUTZPAH

The quality of testing judges' willingness to suspend their disbelief. It is gall carried to a point of magnificent supererogation. (But, like almost any other vice, it has its place.)

An example of unpardonable chutzpah was committed by the lawyer, an experienced labor-management counsel, who had sat through the five or six cases we had heard in our long morning session. We reconvened in the afternoon to hear his case, the final one of the day and a run-of-the-mill one. His opener was: "Since you don't have the time pressure that you had this morning, I suggest that we have ten more minutes."

Another labor-management case produced a memorable argument. Counsel for the employer had sat through one or two other such arguments, where issues were similar, and had developed a good sense of the mood of the court, which he did not overplay. He began, "I'll continue the dialogue." From the briefs we knew that he had a great deal to talk about. The decision of the National Labor Relations Board that we were reviewing was fairly open to serious attack. The lawyer began so dispassionately (a mood rarely encountered in these cases) that I wondered what side he was on. Then, after conceding some unimportant points, he came on strong on the key issue, veritably decimating all support for the Board's decision.

The Board's attorney, a veteran of several decades of jousting in the appellate arena, must have sensed the obvious hostility of an aroused court as she approached the lectern. But she began, "Of course the Board should be affirmed." I had to admire this contemporary analogue of the Charge of the Light Brigade. At the end of argument, we suggested that she convey to her superior our recommendation that she be given a medal of valor.

CLIENT IN COURT

A device which, when calculated to generate sympathy, more often than not backfires.

The most egregious example of this puzzling proclivity of some lawyers occurs when the lawyer broadcasts the presence of his client in the first row. Hardly less diverting is the unannounced but perfectly obvious presence of a client, sometimes hedged about with spouse and children, in a back row. In either case there is likely to be deep frowning, violent head shaking, mutual comforting, and even the frenetic sending of notes down to the counsel table.

The court pays attention, but in a negative way. The judges are burdened with an unnecessary problem – how to press counsel or challenge his argument without demeaning him in the eyes of his client. In one of our cases one of our judges very properly, I thought, criticized counsel for the length of a brief. Later the lawyer upbraided the judge for doing this when – a fact not known to the judge – the client was in court.

I do not mean that clients should not be in court, only that their presence should not be based on tactics or become disconcertingly manifest. Sometimes counsel cannot control whether his client will be in the courtroom. The client may want to be there, and he pays the bills. No matter how hard the lawyer tries to persuade the client that it is not advisable to be present, the client may not listen. Clients may have been so involved in the development of the appeal that they understandably want to see the last act of the drama. In criminal cases, where a jail sentence has been or may be imposed, the defendant's family may want to be present to see whether justice is done. Their presence may not in fact be a device designed by counsel to engender sympathy but a human need of the client's family to see whether the system is fair. It is important in such case that the system try to show that it is.

One such example was a case originally brought by a bright but eccentric individual against his employer. To begin with, like most pro se cases, his cause had been inartfully pleaded, occasioning much wasted motion for himself, his adversary, and the court. It was a good thing, therefore, that he eventually sought counsel, who was a young associate in a reputable firm. Here are my notes of the argument:

> "We are glad that at last we have a brief and argument from a rational professional. But the client is in the front row, leaning on every word, exhibiting a certain amount of body English. We are – or at least I am – very self conscious about *not* wishing to push or be critical of the lawyer's efforts . . . or we'll get a petition to remove him.
>
> "Counsel for appellee, thankfully, was cool, restraining any impulse to engage in any personal criticism of appellant, who obviously has long been a thorn in the side of the

employer.

"The young associate got some good experience. The court got a good brief and argument. The client was well served. This, then, was not just a charade. If there had been a real issue, it would have been uncovered."

Another case also involved an issue of discrimination in employment. Plaintiff was by no means eccentric. But her case led to some highly complex analysis. I think it was good that she was in court to realize that the judges had to reckon with a number of technical requirements affecting the making of a prima facie case, the burden of rebuttal, and the final burden of persuasion. I hope that she left the courtroom with the conviction that the judges were going to decide her case on the basis of principle, not prejudice.

CONFIDENCE

A quality which, however manifested by counsel, if it stems from hard analysis, stands a good chance of spreading its benign influence to the court.
Synonym: ***conviction.***

As my "if" clause reflects, I place substance – having a good case and knowing it backward and forward, knowing the strengths and how to deal with the weaknesses – as both the necessary and the sufficient ingredient of confidence. Usually this quality is exhibited by a lawyer for an appellee, i.e., a lawyer who has already persuaded a judge, a jury, or a governmental agency of the merits of his case. The victory below is something like a suit of armor worn beneath some less essential outer garments. For example, in many appeals in criminal cases an able lawyer for the appellant will speak with considerable force and will argue several issues vigorously. He is good enough to push the court into a state of discomfort. What looked like an easy affirmance is now vulnerable to several attacks.

Then the equally able prosecutor begins coolly, perhaps even boringly, and deals with issue after issue: no objection here, no request for a charge there; several pieces of evidence omitted from appellant's argument add up to sufficient evidence to support the jury's verdict; and, even if the court erred in cutting off the impeaching cross-examination of a key witness, it is harmless error because of a, b, c, d, e, and f. The tight cumulatively overpowering summary of evidence, with page references to the transcript, utterly devastated the key witness and left us in no doubt. The appellee's coat of armor had been resplendently revealed. Once again we had seen the difference in force needed to climb a rope from that needed simply to keep from slipping.

There are also, however, occasions when counsel for an appellant, despite having lost his case at the trial level, comes into court radiating solid confidence and the sweet smell of success. What he has in his arsenal is some egregious error committed by the trial judge. One such example was the hasty action of a trial judge in ruling against a party who had never been served with process and thus had never been brought into the court's jurisdiction.

Another such confident appellant came into court having all

the law from a number of courts on his side. For some reason the trial judge, an excellent one, had been persuaded that these cases were not applicable. Viewed with the perspective of time and a complete survey of the law on point, appellant's weapons now look deadly and appellee's armor seems now to have more chinks than links. In such cases the appellant's counsel has the rare opportunity to ask for reversal as one who speaks "more in sorrow than in anger."

Occasionally a case involving two private parties will go to decision before a governmental body realizes that a broad public policy issue is at stake. It will then belatedly ask permission to file a brief as "friend of the court" (amicus curiae). By the time the case reaches the appellate court, its context and scope have changed so much as not to be recognizable. Here, too, a losing party below, armed with the powerful support of the amicus, may often come into court radiating unusual confidence.

Although any lawyer, whether for appellant or appellee, armed with a good case, thoroughly prepared on the law, the facts, and policy implications, must inevitably reflect an ineffable but almost palpable sense of confidence, whatever may be his skills in speaking or his "presence," it is also true that substance can be aided by manner. Manner without substance will not do; but manner and substance will do better than substance alone.

By manner I do not mean artificially fabricated mannerisms but rather style in the sense used by Buffon when he wrote, "Le style, c'est l'homme meme." Manner is the composite of language, posture, pace, tone, facial expression, eye contact, gestures . . . all the ways in which an advocate's thoughts and emotional intensities become conveyed to others.

In my catalogue of counsel I find three profiles illustrating different levels of confidence-stimulating manner. The first is that of a young attorney who, despite a Rip Van Winkle arrival in the courtroom after we had instructed counsel for appellee to begin argument and despite having at best an indifferent case, made a strong and favorable impression. My notes read: "He knew the cases, spoke rapidly, was intense. He was persistent, somewhat like a raw primeval force. When he came to difficult precedents, he would not try to distinguish them, but merely said they were wrong. He pitched his argument to an extreme position. He did not try to make decision easy for the court." This young attorney had a presence and personality which, when he would add the judgment gained from experience, would be compelling.

A second character was an older man, an individual practitioner. My notes read: "Speaks slowly, bumblingly, but gives us the feeling that he knows the field. Has a cold so his gruff assertions may be more cryptic than usual. When one of us put to him a hypothetical question together with a suggested answer that looked as if it might be damaging, his reply was simply, 'It seems to me to be sensible. I can't say more than that,' and the court accepts." In other words, so impressive were the rough-hewn integrity and judgment of this lawyer that the answer no longer appeared damaging; the testing attempted by one of us judges suddenly appeared to be merely cute. Thus can a manner stemming from inner character, mellowed by judgment, smooth the way for its possessor. In this particular case this lawyer was also aided by the contrasting image of his adversary as to which my notes read: "Lackluster. No sense of conviction. He is like a bean bag; punch him here and he yields only to bulge somewhere else."

Perhaps my third personage reflects the summum bonum of the confidence factor of advocacy. For in this lawyer were combined a controlled passion, the judgment gained from long experience, and a touch of art. This last ingredient took the form of drawing on some of the many cases he had argued before us, making a few salient comparisons, inducing us to feel that we and he had shared many battles, then, without stepping over the line into presumptuousness or unctuousness, conveying to the judges that he was taking them into his confidence. The result of this combination of earnestness, experience, and elegance is that whether the advocate wins his case or not (he won this one), every judge listens with rapt attention and gives the argument his most thorough consideration.

CONTROL (and its loss)

The ability to give some direction to the discussion of issues. This could be subtitled control of time, of self, of court, or of argument.

Given the facts that the allotted time is brief, perhaps 15 minutes; that a certain amount of time must be spent on factual and procedural background; and that three or more judges are in various stages of ignorance and with diverse interests to pursue via sometimes awkward, lengthy, repetitive, and irrelevant questions . . . and sometimes terribly acute, pointed, and lethal ones, the area of possible control is about equivalent to that of an astronaut on a satellite orbiting mission. He may invoke his ingenuity to attempt to arrest malfunctioning and, when disaster threatens, may use manual controls to bring about an emergency landing. But in the main his course is determined by others.

After hearing and participating in hundreds of oral case presentations, the closest I can come to a formula for retaining some minimal degree of control is this: be thoroughly prepared on facts, law, policy, legislative history, scholarly commentary; start the presentation with as brief a background statement as possible, getting to the high ground of major point-making as soon as possible; then relax a bit when the questions come and answer the first few thoroughly but concisely; then consult your mental checkoff list to see what priority matters must at all costs be addressed and use all your ingenuity to save a few minutes to address them.

One specific technique, suggested to me by a veteran advocate, is at the very outset to list the points one hopes to make. "Generally, one judge will remember near the end of the argument that I ticked off three points at the beginning and, if I have gotten sidetracked and only have had the opportunity to discuss one or two of those points, that judge will ask before the argument ends or even after time has expired if I would at least discuss briefly the third point."

So to prescribe is easy; how to do it, particularly how to fend off derailing questions and gracefully get back to some key issues, is an art; it cannot be learned through teaching but through observation and experience.

It is well to realize at the outset that the burden of retaining

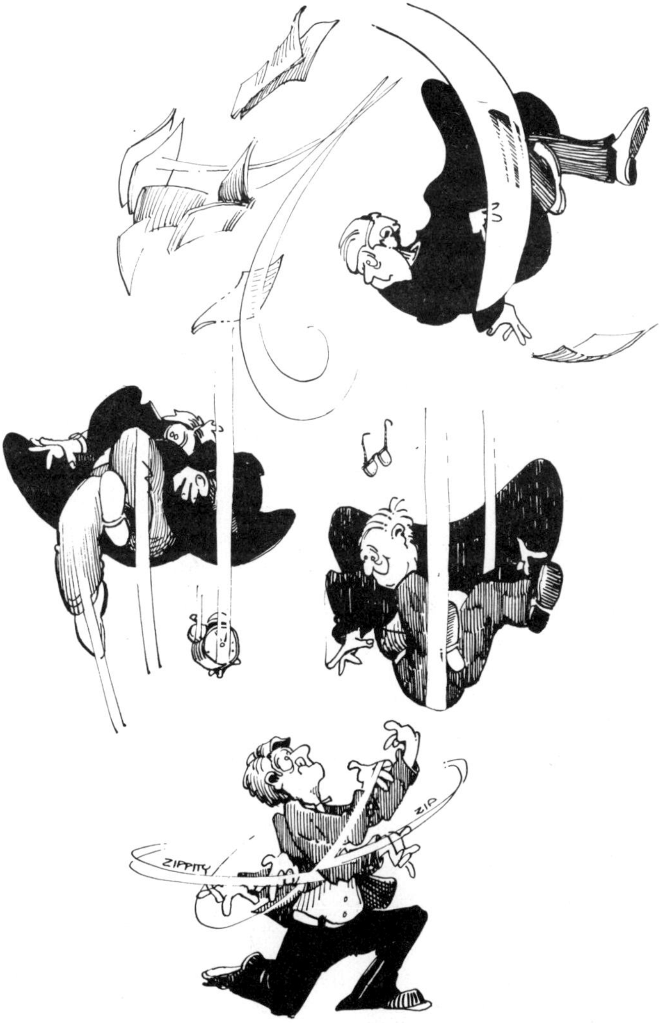

some minimal degree of control differs as between appellant and appellee. Appellant comes to court with an uphill road to travel; he cannot relax after making one point but must attend to others; he cannot assume that the silence of judges means agreement with his cause. Appellee, however, is able to sit through his adversary's ordeal, see what issues have interested the judges, sense which ones have had enough discussion, and address only those on which he thinks the court needs some added perspective, facts, authorities, or reasoning. If he has reasonable intuition, he can sense when he has said enough to satisfy the judges; he then can stop, ask if there is anything else that the court is interested in, and sit down.

This much said, it is nevertheless a truism applicable to counsel on both sides that insofar as controlling time is concerned the dice are loaded against the advocate.

All I can hope to do here is to extract from my notes a few memories of things done badly and things done well. I begin with a litany of misadventures.

Chronologically first and all too frequent is the wasted start. This is ironic since the first five minutes are perhaps the easiest to control. Unless a judge comes loaded for bear and can hardly wait for counsel to address the court before he pops his cherished question, this is the time when the judges are reviewing their notes, flipping through the briefs, and generally settling in. Yet instead of exploiting this opportunity to the limit and making as much mileage as possible, counsel perversely will spend precious minutes on nonessential facts and in making the most minute corrections in their briefs, as if to indicate the extraordinarily high altitude of their integrity.

In one argument, for which a young counsel for appellant had been given twenty minutes, I noted at the end of fifteen minutes that he had not gotten through a very pedestrian accounting of the rather unremarkable facts. With six difficult issues to address, his presentation soon became a shambles. Much harder to understand was the veteran Washington lawyer who had held important positions in government. At first he radiated both confidence and authority but he was trapped by his desire to display expertise, for he wasted both valuable time and the opportunity to make an impact at the very beginning by loading us with rather meaningless exhibits, supposed aids to argument.

Being over-tense creates its own problems but being over-relaxed is also a hazard, a cause, when it exists, of loss of control. One's very competence, poise, and familiarity with the court can lead one to be too thorough in presenting facts, too discursive and perfectionist in discussing each issue. One can too easily lose oneself in the joy of polished discourse before an appreciative forum and lose all track of time.

The unwary advocate walks through a mine field of appellate argument. The metaphor is apt, for certain errors of omission or commission perform like activated mines; they explode and galvanize the court's attention, often for the duration of the argument. Once I witnessed a lawyer who I knew to be generally careful being hoist by his own petard for quoting a treatise for a proposition without including a qualifying footnote. The judge who had discovered this gaffe had been irrevocably lost. Another time a lawyer was going along swimmingly in attacking an evidentiary ruling, but came to grief when he could not give the transcript reference showing when and precisely how counsel had raised his objection, if indeed he had said anything at all. The context had become critical. All the judges chimed in. What began as an effective assault quickly became a chaotic rout. In other cases counsel's loss of control began with the omission of a key fact, commencing argument on a minor issue, a concession on some issues that should never have been contested in the first place, failure to recognize a recent and highly relevant case authority, an attempt to bring in some new issue, and even the classic failure to make sure that cases one is strongly relying on have not been overruled or tagged for certiorari review by the Supreme Court. Perhaps this comes down to saying that although good lawyering may not assure the lawyer control of his time, the absence of good lawyering is an invitation to intervention from the bench.

Even if counsel has gotten off to a strong crisp start and has exhibited no foible of craftsmanship, there comes the time when one judge asks a question and perhaps asks it again in different words; then another judge asks his; and a third judge, who has been patiently waiting, now claims his turn. Meanwhile, one's remaining time has shrunk to five minutes or less, and issues that one knows are crucial ones have not been discussed. Lawyers who know what to do under this circumstance in order gracefully to regain control of their time have mastered one of the major challenges of oral presentation. Experience, unhappily, is not a reliable teacher, if I may cite my notes of two highly regarded lawyers and their loss of control in two important appeals.

The first incident illustrates the importance of keeping one's mental list of priorities in mind from the first question asked by a judge. My notation reads, "Like a military commander without any sense of high strategy, he felt that every question from the court, even though off the mark, had to be answered exhaustively. This left him without time for the big issues." The second incident points to the moral that one's sense of priorities should really begin with one's written brief. Here is my reaction to his presentation:

> "He has written a terribly overblown, oversize brief which has set all judges' teeth on edge. The very length of his brief may have disabled him from handling a compressed oral argument. He is buried under questions; new ones are asked before old ones are answered. Judges could be more restrained but the case is important and issues look close; in such a case we are physically uncomfortable so long as we see stones to turn over, points to be cleared up. Counsel in this situation needs to think like a newsman – to begin with the most comprehensive topic sentence; if he is cut off, he should have his most important statement behind him."

When time has run out, an advocate has several options. The first, and by no means a bad one, is to sit down, since very few souls are saved in an overtime argument. But if one is in the middle of an answer to a judge, even if one wishes the question had not been asked, it is less than prepossessing to say as did one counsel with all too obvious relief, "I see my time's up." Perhaps the worst course is for counsel to pretend that he has not seen the clock or the red light and continue cavalierly into overtime. What counsel does not realize is how quickly revulsion rises in one or all of the judges, effectively stopping the listening function. Still another course is to ask for more time. This should be followed with the greatest sensitivity. One lawyer, having stirred my admiration with his economy of words and careful argument, asked and received added time, which he proceeded to squander on an insignificant issue already conceded by his opponent. I had to tell him that he had made a great argument until three minutes ago, but would he now "please sit down."

Since there are few absolutes in appellate advocacy, it will not be surprising if I say that there are times when overtime must be sought. If judges have used a great deal of counsel's time with questions, and if because of or despite such colloquy there remain untouched some important points, counsel should say something like, "Your Honors, I see my time is up. I feel that I should speak briefly to the questions __________ and __________. Might I have two minutes?" I think it would be a rare court that would deny such a request. Indeed, I recall an effective advocate who had used his time well but was unable to cover all his terrain. When the red light went on, he simply stopped in the middle of a sentence. Of course we asked him to conclude as he saw fit; he did not have to ask for time.

Although I cannot give any sure-fire formula for retaining minimum control of argument time, I can pass on a few examples of what I considered superb performance. One of the appellate lawyers whom I respect the most is a young woman. After one argument I wrote these impressions:

> "When she is appellee, she begins with something relevant to what has engaged the attention of the court in the argument of her adversary. She will correct facts and make her points in a crisp, tough, no-nonsense way, but without being personally insulting or snide. She radiates confidence in her case. She *uses* questions, not only to answer them, but to move on to another point. This time she addressed what had been the major subject of colloquy until one judge said he did not need any more discussion on that point. Then, talking at a good clip, not wasting a word, in command of facts, able to discuss any cited case, left alone by the judges after a few sallies, she runs beautifully like a thoroughbred filly on the home stretch."

Another attorney, a young lawyer from the Department of Justice, was competent, low key, conversational, persuasive. He distinguished hypotheticals with the simple, but in this case fair preface, "Not this case." He did not detain us. He closed after ten minutes, having five to spare. This had been a good example of how much, even with an active bench, a good advocate can pack into ten minutes.

An older attorney, in his fifties, comes to us with a reputation not so much of brilliance, but of integrity and solidity. He exploits this by a measured pace, resonant voice impassively detailing the facts. He is a steam roller, not a racer nor an elegant Mercedes. He dealt with our overactive judges, after handling their questions for fifteen minutes, by saying, "I would, if I may, devote my remaining time to an issue about which nothing has been said." He was left in peace, without any feeling of resentment on the part of the judges.

Other notes of successful coping include the Labor Board attorney who began by conceding some minor points without exposing any key argument to vulnerability, selected a few points for argument and moved on nicely, concluding with "if the court has no further questions"; the experienced woman advocate who, when a judge chided her saying "You haven't answered my question," replied with composure and fairness, "Well, Your Honor, I intended to. Perhaps you can help me understand where I have not"; and the attorney who, being badgered by time-wasting questions, nodded at the five minute warning light and said, "Let me go to the other point."

CREDIBILITY
(a misplaced argument)

This is an argument that the testimony of a key witness is so unbelievable that the verdict or judgment below must be reversed. While an obviously proper argument to make to the finder of fact, it is almost never justified at the appellate level.

Although some issues concerning the proper standard of review are highly technical, the standard governing the reviewability of factual judgments on the part of triers of fact (administrative law judges, trial judges, juries, agency officials) is not. It is simply that if there is sufficient evidence which, *if believed*, could support a rational decision, the conclusion stands. To demonstrate that a witness could not be believed, one needs ammunition of rare caliber – flat internal contradictions, documentary proof that the witness could not have observed, etc.

I am almost embarrassed to repeat something that any law student of more than a month's matriculation knows. My excuse lies in incidents like the following:

> After repeated questioning, a mid-career solo practitioner still did not understand that where evidence is conflicting, the trial judge can, indeed, must choose.
>
> In a labor case, the company's lawyer, a veteran out-of-circuit practitioner, knew better but was forced to make credibility arguments. He tried, unsuccessfully, to look as if

his heart was in it.

In a similar case, the company attorney from a small firm insisted that we review the Labor Board's factual findings as if they were questions of law. This one fought like a terrier to the end.

In a case arising out of an industrial accident, the employer was appealing a determination by the Secretary of Labor. My notes: "The facade is impressive: pin stripe suit, blue tie, white dots. Radiates crispness, competence. But there is less here than meets the eye. In trying to reverse an Administrative Law Judge, he says, 'only issues of credibility are involved.'"

Finally, a single argument produced two of my favorite exchanges between judge and advocate. The issue on appeal was whether a defendant had made a voluntary and knowing plea of guilty.

Judge: "Didn't the judge find that defendant had not taken drugs at the time of the plea?"

Counsel: "Yes, Your Honor, but defendant testified to the contrary." (!)

Counsel: "Defendant's psychologist said defendant was a paranoid schizophrenic."

Judge: "Yes, but didn't the government's psychiatrist say he was a chronic schizophrenic?"

Counsel: "Yes, they both agreed." (!)

DANCER

An advocate who believes that he can infuse strength into an otherwise flaccid case by substituting body dynamics for the spoken word.

Notice that I did not say that he relies on body motion to supplement or emphasize a point but that he relies on it as a substitute. Not that he intends it that way. But when he warms up and moves from one side of the lectern to the other, flailing his arms, twisting his body, and dancing lightly on his feet like a boxer, I have long since lost track of what he is saying, so fascinated am I with his gyrations.

A refined form of dancing is that involving only use of the hands. This kind of engaging, perhaps overengaging, lawyer is likely to remind one of a pastry cook because, as he works into his argument, his hands are working into some invisible dough which he kneads rhythmically, accompanying all this with a beaming, expectant smile. He also uses his fingers to count, point, spread, and interlock; he uses fists to clench and pound; and he extends his palms up, down, and sideways. I soon come to the point where I either look at him and admire the manual ballet or look down at the bench and do what I'm paid to do, listen to the argument.

Demonstrative Evidence

Visual aids to argument; devices suitable for a salesmen's meeting, but seldom for an appellate argument.

Some advocates, reasoning that people in general seem to understand both the written and the spoken word less and less, conclude that charts, graphs, symbols can blaze the shortest trail to judges' minds. But perhaps because judges are prisoners of their own conventions, the introduction of any innovative ploy in presentation causes a certain amount of wheel spinning and lost motion as the judges realize that they have something in addition to the briefs and oral remarks of counsel to attend to.

One very reputable lawyer who had already favored us with a "brief" very much oversize unaccountably thought he was doing himself and us a service by distributing to us on the morning of argument a 25 page "outline" of what he was going to say.

On another occasion a lawyer thoughtfully posted on a blackboard several charts presenting complicated statistics in a case involving an electric utility. Whatever clarity had been achieved from reading the briefs quickly dissipated as the lawyer began to explain the charts, misspeak himself, correct himself, start over, and forever lose himself at the first silly question of an utterly confused judge. I could think only of the comedic chaos of Robert Benchly presenting his "Treasurer's Report."

For me the high point in the use of demonstrative evidence in appellate advocacy was reached in a patent case. The invention at issue was not a complex one of the Rube Goldberg variety but, at least in hindsight, a very simple one. The advocate, wishing to drive home the point that at times the most creative concepts are the simplest, narrated the story, apocryphal or not, of Columbus demonstrating with the utmost simplicity how he could make an egg stand on end, i.e., by cracking one end slightly so that it presented a sufficient surface to rest on. The lawyer, with a flourish, produced a brown paper bag, announced its contents – an egg – and proceeded to tap the bottom. The tap being ineffective, the egg continued to roll on its side. The lawyer, a bit reddened, increased his force. As the impassive, incredulous judges watched, they saw the intractable egg continue to roll irresponsibly. Finally, the frustrated advocate, throwing caution to the winds, administered such a coup de gras – or coup d'oeuf – that not only a bit of the bottom shell but the entire egg fairly exploded, spattering the clerk's bench and a very surprised and discomfited clerk of court. I completely forget what

happened thereafter, including, of course, the argument.

Once again, as so often in these commentaries, I abjure any absolutist proscription. These *are* times when visual aids to argument make a great deal of sense. A map in a land condemnation case, a blown-up chart in an admiralty case, a cutaway model of a device in a patent case . . . these obviously have an advantage over the power of words which, after all, cannot felicitously describe a circular staircase.

DILETTANTE

An advocate who, solely because of his family's position in a firm, inherited or married wealth, or past political prominence, has sufficient clientele to thrust him into an appellate court.

This kind of lawyer possesses all the characteristics one could wish: an impressive, pleasant bearing; excellent yet easy diction; knowledge of legal principles, historic cases, and esoteric bits of information about eminent judges, law professors, and commentators. Somehow, the notes struck by all these hammers are just a little bit off key. The factual presentation is likely to be interesting, even diverting, but unorganized, and leading nowhere. The discussion of cases is likely to be conclusory and cavalier; sometimes it becomes all too apparent that the advocate is not remotely acquainted with the leading cases. If this performer's clients happen to be in the back of the courtroom, they may well believe that they have received good value for their money, for the judges, being moved by a sense of charity at the spectacle of tragic miscasting, have not asked embarrassing questions. But they look upon the exercise as posturing, not serious advocacy.

Dishrag

An advocate whose smart texture of crisp linen, upon being dampened by bench inquiries, loses all stiffening and form.

This is a vexing type, because the judges know that this lawyer possesses experience, knowledge, judgment. They look to him earnestly for help beyond what the briefs have given. A judge trying to be helpful puts a hypothetical case that can easily be distinguished from that being argued. The advocate, perhaps from some deeply rooted dislike of controversy, simply concedes the similarity and relevance of the hypothetical. The judge silently gnashes his teeth.

Earnestness (emotional over-involvement)

The characteristics of conduct reflecting an advocate's personal belief in the merits of his client's cause, emotional over-involvement being an exaggerated degree of earnestness.

When earnestness is linked with and based upon a rigorous analysis of one's case, it is identical to the sense of confidence that we have discussed. When earnestness is not so supported but is rather exuded only as a disembodied perfume, it will generally prove no substitute for law or facts. Nevertheless, it being considered an admirable trait to believe in one's client's cause, a perception of earnestness by the judges will accomplish one valuable objective: it will assure that an argument will be seriously considered. This is to be contrasted with the dishrag syndrome we have discussed: although a dishrag response to questions may cause one to lose a case that one shouldn't, earnestness tends to guarantee that one will not lose such a case. I call this disciplined emotional involvement.

But emotional over-involvement is quite a different matter. I cannot remember ever considering it a positive factor. It is to oral presentation as bright red paint is to an authentic Chippendale chair, irrelevant, hard to remove, and disconcerting. One kind of over-involvement stems from close association with one's client. The paradigm of such a case is where an individual represents himself, is pleading his cause pro se. When a judge puts a hard question to such an advocate, it very often provokes a venting of pent-up emotions, either a blow-up or a break-down. But even a professional lawyer occasionally becomes too closely entwined with his client's life and hopes. In one such case, my notes read: "Appellant's counsel is sincere, intense, and angry. He is very close to his client. He should give chapter and verse where the district court went wrong, rather than play to the galleries, in this case, his client."

Another kind of emotional disablement, a common one, comes from being oversold on one's case. This leads to exaggerated rhetoric as these samples from my notes show. Bucking a Labor Board finding in a routine case, counsel was "very smooth

and ultra-emphatic, as if this were terribly shocking. I found myself saying out loud that the only words I found to describe this run-of-the-mill situation were 'Ho' and 'Hum.'" A second counsel, trying to get a new civil trial, didn't give basic facts but leaped into his legal argument. The judges had to pull out the information. "He was overemphatic in an uphill fight. He pointed to the bench with a white pen as if he were teaching children (perhaps he was closer to the mark than I thought)." Possibly a synthetic kind of emotionalism is simply the advocate's style of address as these observations record: "His advocacy consists of getting red in the face, inflating, and gesticulating wildly with eyes closed"; a young woman assistant attorney general "was competent but shrill and indignant; she does not make me happy to be on her side"; a male attorney in his mid forties from a big firm "is shrill to the point of obfuscation"; a solo practitioner of mature years "is not stupid but eccentric and almost incomprehensible. Uses violent hand gestures. Speaks in raised, squeaky, intense tone. Yet once in a while carries some conviction."

An identifiable sub-type of the emotionally over-involved counsel is that which I call the High Tension Wire. He feels so strongly about his case (apparently every case) that the electricity of vehemence throbs so loudly that I cannot hear the words. Not that he rages and shouts, but he is so obviously boiling inside that my whole focus is on whether and when he will explode.

Finally, emotional over-involvement not infrequently is a result of counsel's association with a case over such a long time that all his restraint, reserve, resilience, perspective, and manners have long since been shredded to bits. Here is how an important, long-lived case appeared to me after oral argument:

> "A case out of control, exhibiting a pair of lawyers that would challenge Daumier. Appellant is a tall, slender, pasty, sly serpent – a senior partner in a large firm. Appellee, also a senior in a big firm, is shorter – a raging bull. The first read from typed pages in a notebook and smiled like the Cheshire cat when he thought he was making points. He was trying to portray his client, a big corporation, as being injured innocence itself, being exploited by irresponsible tactics of opposing counsel. As one of the judges pressed him on his client's footdragging and other such tactics, he lost momentum, and any sense of convictions. Appellee, in trying to show that his client was sweet reasonableness itself was his own worst argument. As he fulminated, thrusting pejorative darts at his opponent in every sentence, he made us pity the poor trial judge who had to deal with him. This prompted me to ask: 'When able lawyers so distrust each other, how can courts help?' This was a serious insult, but he was so wrapped up in his venom and rhetoric that he didn't realize it."

EMPHASIS

The differentiation given words by one's voice and bearing, which is one of the justifications for oral presentations.

Having just delivered myself of several homilies concerning overemphasis, I add quickly that underemphasis or the absence of emphasis is also a sin, deadlier for the judges if not for counsel.

Most of the time, it is safe to say, the epitome of underemphasis is the advocate who, having written a brief, either reads the brief verbatim or writes another version of it and reads that. Somehow in that unfortunate situation, the decibel count does not substitute for emphasis. I have dim memories of attorneys with almost inaudible voices who have read atonally and of those like the lawyer in the following note: "Loud, glib, harried. At 1:12 p.m. after a long morning of five cases, I reflect, 'How unintelligible, especially when one is tired.' But there was more to come. The United States Attorney argued. My notes at 1:30, 'Typical, thorough, competent, dull." Sometimes all it takes is a reminder to counsel that we would like a more animated argument. And a rather surefire expedient is to begin to ask questions; if counsel are prepared, their extemporaneous answers make far better listening than reading from a script.

I do, however, remember one occasion when a woman lawyer read an entire argument that was eminently listenable. I do not know her secret and would not attempt to prescribe a formula for successful reading. I mention this fact only as another instance of the nonexistence of a rule of conduct in oral preparation that does not have its exceptions.

EXCELLENCE

Not a single quality but the impression resulting from the mix of qualities – all good – of an advocate.

Just as Justice Stewart referred to obscenity, I cannot define excellence but I know it when I see it. All my expectations from argument have been realized. The lawyer has done all he possibly could for his client and has also eased the task of the judges as much as he could.

I devote a single heading to "excellence," despite my inability to define it, and despite the fact that examples of excellence will be found under many other headings, simply because I want to underscore that it exists not infrequently. Although I shall not try to give the same amount of time to excellence as I give to foibles and follies, I want to set down a few examples to memoralize not only its frequent presence but the varieties of its coloration.

Sometimes when all other relevant competences are present, the added factor of long experience adds a very special flavor. Item – "A Labor Board veteran. He knows his record and his memory of the law is long. He refers to a case he argued before this court before any sitting judge had joined the court."

Sometimes a lawyer has what could be called, justly, a commanding presence. Here is my memory of a lawyer for a utility defending a judgment below against the Commissioner of Internal Revenue: "You have confidence in him. He does not look devious. He eased me. Free of notes. Tackles government's strongest argument. Speaks with authority. Puts lid on questions (i.e., doesn't let them get out of hand). Responsive. Has time to spare. What more can one ask?"

But a commanding presence is not necessary. Item – "Young attorney. Quiet, knowledgable, thoughtful. One judge presses him, indicating that he is persuaded by his adversary's argument. The attorney gives a compelling answer. The case, in my mind, and I think in the minds of my colleagues, is easy from this point on. Indeed, the judges' conference proved to be very cursory." Item – In a criminal appeal the assistant United States Attorney was "not commanding. But sets the record straight in identifying 'facts' alluded to by appellants which were *not* of record. Is responsive and resilient and has a winning attitude of reasonableness." Item – "A superb, humble, serious, low-key, responsive, reasonable, relevant, well-prepared, succinct public interest lawyer."

Among other things excellence means doing what is necessary to put one's case in its strongest light, and no more. The following argument description might not result in any Oscar for the appellee, but seems to me to qualify for excellence:

> "Appellant comes to argument fortified by a monumental brief. Counsel is young, bright-eyed, bushy-tailed but lackluster, with no emphasis. His argument is abstract, doesn't seem to fit the key facts. His oral argument doesn't convey the impression of serious error.
>
> "Appellee is a dour, weathered woman veteran of many a similar battle. She has sat at counsel table like a patient cobra awaiting the time to strike at the pitiful rabbit playing in front of it. She speaks briefly and pungently – referring, in a manner that her hearers are led to receive as reasonable, to the case as 'egregious.' Then stops. She handles the few

questions crisply. Somehow, whatever aura of close contest was created by the appellant's oversize brief has been dissipated."

My final sampling is that of a lawyer who, because of his excellence, won a case he might not have won had he been less effective or had the contest been a more even one. He came to argument wearing the invisible cloak of a reputation for past competence and integrity. He proceeded in a low-key, confident way, identifying the vulnerable point in the government-appellee's case and distinguishing compellingly every legal authority cited by the government. The opposition was not incompetent but only mediocre. After losing the appeal the government mounted a massive effort to secure a rehearing, turning in a far stronger brief than the earlier one. We held fast. I think we reached a sound result but I acknowledge that if effort at trial on the part of the government had been of the quality of its memorandum supporting rehearing, we might have decided the other way. So good lawyering does count.

BIG FISH OUT OF WATER

An advocate with far-flung reputation, perhaps deserved, in his field, but with no discernible aptitude for dealing effectively with an appellate court.

For some reason hidden to me, very substantial and sophisticated clients, who include both individuals and corporations, after being served by obviously competent lawyers in complex litigation, will not only retain new counsel to handle their appeal, but will choose a lawyer solely because of the name recognition factor.

Thus it was that in a very significant business case involving many corporations and governmental bodies one of the major parties was represented by a nationally known trial lawyer whose sensational cases had long made the headlines. Here is my then-recorded impression: "He is out of his field. He is rather pathetic, not being very relevant and covering trite points. He has fans in the courtroom. His network has passed the word for young people to come and hear the great advocate. There are no questions. It is embarrassing to anyone who knows what the case is all about."

When we were favored on another occasion with a celebrity, my rather acerbic note read: "engaging – a bit rhetorical – name dropper (referring to his big cases) . . . but poor brief (he is above that sort of thing)."

I conclude this rather jaundiced treatment of "big fish" by saying that the really big fish, who has not only earned his reputation but continues to deserve it and whose acuteness therefore enables him to assess the particular challenges of a new forum, swims superbly even in unfamiliar waters. My Exhibit A of such a counsel is the Washington lawyer, celebrated for his trial work, who came in on the appeal of an unsuccessful defendant in a tax evasion case. The brief was highly competent. This was gratifying but what was really surprising was the lawyer's intimate knowledge of a lengthy and complex record of a case he had never tried. This was professionalism at its best.

FADING FOLIAGE

The senior partner who has lingered too long. He glows at first, but drops all too soon.

The big fish who finds himself out of water in an appellate court is temporarily pathetic, but we can hope he can return to his old and happier haunts. The lawyer, however, whom aging has not treated kindly presents an unrelievedly pathetic picture. The judges, remembering years of highly competent work, are gentle. Opposing counsel is predictably respectful. The younger associate, who wrote the brief and sits at counsel table, is acutely uncomfortable. Here is one camera shot of such a travesty:

"He has 25 minutes in this important securities case. He uses the first four or five in correcting pages of his brief. Then he begins, steadfastly looking down at the lectern, occasionally favoring the court with a look over his glasses. This was incredibly dull. Our interest was never lost because it was never attracted in the first place. To occupy my mind at one point, I looked at the lectern to see what he was reading. There was nothing there!

"He did not know the number of shares involved in the transaction at issue nor the effect of the transaction on the price of shares. A judge had done some simple arithmetic which seemed to blow him out of the water. He had no response. Then, when the red light came on, he continued blandly. After the exhibition ended, one of my colleagues said, 'Counsel, since you will be arguing other cases, you must not waste time as you did today.' This was a dressing down that one might expect to be given to a neophyte . . . but not a senior partner of a large firm!!!"

I can only hope that the client *was* in the courtroom to see what its sizeable counsel fees were paying for.

THE GASCON

An advocate who, from overweening confidence in his case or from a chronic suicidal complex, throws caution and diplomacy to the winds, draws his sword and takes on all judges at once.

I am not insensible to the attractive qualities of Cyrano de Bergerac and the Three Musketeers. Indeed, I find myself at times in a state of reluctant admiration when I see their modern counterpart in an appellate courtroom. My unheard internal aside is, "This is spectacular but how much easier counsel could make his job . . . and ours."

I know of one lawyer who is encyclopedic in his knowledge of applicable law, who puts everything he has into both his trial work and his appellate work, who has won his share of hard cases and therefore comes into court with the respect, both grudging and ungrudging, of our judges. But inevitably he places a chip on his shoulder and keeps it there while he essentially dares the court to hold against him. Being human, we are tempted to accept his challenge.

Another lawyer, representing a state government against which a state prisoner is seeking a writ of habeas corpus, almost always comes to us having won the case perhaps several times in state court (at trial, or on appeal to the state's supreme court, and possibly in a post-conviction proceeding) and in the federal trial court. This is, of course, impressive armor, of which we are acutely aware. But that is not enough for counsel, who instructs us very didactically as to what our very limited function is. Indeed, the clear impression we receive is that the case shouldn't be before us and that we are ninnies in not having thrown it out long ago and saved counsel some valuable time. Again, being human, we may, in a weak moment, be tempted to find a chink in this armor.

Here is my post-argument note of one such argument:

> "Able counsel, but irritatingly bland – as if *all* arguments were frivolous. Is rather hurt if we suggest that an argument has some substance. She uses only five of her fifteen minutes. Usually this is a good tactic, but here I thought she was not doing her job but leaving everything up to us."

HARE

An advocate who is well prepared and assumes that the court is as thoroughly conversant with all of the facts and law as he is. He therefore tries to cover as much ground as possible by (a) talking very rapidly, (b) making great leaps from issue to issue, or (c) doing both.

This character in our bestiary underscores the importance of counsel's getting a sense of the court's level of comprehension of the case. Sometimes, perhaps because the issue is simple or because the court has been striving with the same issue in other cases, the court will indeed be on counsel's level and will be able to follow the most sophisticated argument. However, there is both the danger of assuming that the court knows more than it does, and the antipodal danger of assuming it knows nothing, when in fact the judges have read the briefs and do have a good idea of facts, issues, and pertinent law.

In general, however, a rapid-fire delivery sustained for fifteen or twenty minutes precludes changes in emphasis, prevents good arguments from sinking in, discourages questions, and either exhausts the judges or leaves them far behind. An argument in a drug conspiracy case by such a fast-paced lawyer sounded something like this: "Then Betty said to Joe that Harry had some stuff to sell. Gustave then drove Joe to Albert's house and Ignatz called . . ." This advocate was in complete command of the facts –

which is a good thing – and was time-conscious – another good thing – but assumed we knew the names and numbers of all the players and had total recall – a bad thing.

House Counsel
(Away from Home)

A lawyer who serves as the permanent "inside" legal adviser to a corporation. Because of the high fees charged by the major law firms, many corporations are said to be utilizing house counsel more and more. But it is a rare "inside" adviser who is also a good "outside" advocate.

It is no insult to able house counsel, trial lawyers, or tax experts to say that the peculiar disciplines, constraints, and opportunities of oral presentation to appellate panels to not easily lend themselves to mastery by those who work in other vineyards.

Perhaps just one example will show what can happen:

> "A big commercial case. A big company uses its house counsel, a man in his fifties. Obviously a good counsellor, he is completely out of his element. He does not know he is to stand at the lectern. He speaks like a scholar, not an advocate – yet with authority, until he loses his cool. He gradually works himself up into a froth of indignation, sharing the feelings his corporate client would have if it could feel. He is reduced to stammering that his opponents are playing 'a shell game.' He had to be told his time was up."

JUDGES

Lawyers who were once advocates, whose job now is to decide among advocates, and who, in the process of deciding, will advocate their positions to their colleagues. Judges have the power to make oral presentations a shambles or a stimulating aid to expeditious and sound decisions.

In addition to the substance of their cases, counsel must consider the personalities, quiddities, abilities, predilections, habits and ways of the judges. I am sure than an experienced appellate advocate could catalogue a long list of judges and their idiosyncrasies that would make a literary complement to Daumier's ruthlessly revealing drawings. I am not about to attempt such an unveiling. What I can do is to indicate the kinds of ways in which all of us fall short of the mark of the ideal appellate audience or occasionally live up to it.

First, the foibles which fairly characterize us from time to time. Being human, we are subject to all of them. The saving grace is that on a multi-judge court, each judge will not have the same foible at the same time; indeed, foibles of different judges often offset each other.

Un- or Underprepared – Sometimes a judge has not read a brief or memo, or his reading has been too hasty to be illuminating. In such a predicament, if he is silent, he makes no contribu-

tion to anyone's understanding. But if he asks questions, he actively prevents the oral argument from being the aid to decision that it could be. Long, agonizing minutes will be wasted supplying information that everybody else knows.

Overprepared – Occasionally a judge will be so intrigued by a case in advance of argument that he will read everything very thoroughly, may even do independent research, and will have developed his views very strongly. When this happens, it is a judge of rare restraint who will not allow himself to parade his knowledge just a little bit, and perhaps a little bit more. The result is not necessarily to advance understanding of the particular case. Questions are likely to be ultra-sophisticated, the answers not being relevant to decision.

Clever – A judge may be supremely pleased with himself for coming upon a point that is important. He brings the matter up, and receives a concise answer. Having nothing more to ask, he is likely to ask the same question in different words. And so time runs. I call this the terrier syndrome and dealing with it is one of the meatiest challenges to the lawyer.

Stupid – Judges have blind spots. Being otherwise sophisticated about an awesome range of issues, they will occasionally draw a blank in a particular case. Or it may just be a bad day, when comprehension comes slowly. Or the judge may have some tormenting problem on his mind and his inner turmoil is belied by his outward visage of wisdom and serenity. Therefore, absolutely stupid questions can be asked. I have, for example, asked what I thought was a shrewd question; my only problem was that I had the parties entirely mixed up in my mind. The question made no sense at all. The problem for counsel in such straits is to give a sufficient answer, somehow suggesting the question's stupidity while at the same time avoiding too blatant a disrobing of the judge.

Biting – Judges occasionally erupt in biting criticism that digs deeper than mere debate on issues. Often it is perfectly justified criticism. Perhaps very new, or very old, or disadvantaged counsel may be forgiven gross errors of judgment or breaches of etiquette, but professionals of any stature, earning more than a good living, must not be surprised when judges make an effort to prevent the standards of oral presentation in their courtroom from eroding. Sometimes, however, the criticism stems from a partial view taken by a judge. He may be affronted by what he considers an entirely frivolous argument from reputable counsel. He may make some cutting remark, only to discover some perfectly rational justification for the argument. The criticism was unjustified and, unless the the judge confesses error, an impression of unfairness remains.

Partisan – Once in a while a judge comes to argument with his slip – his bias – showing. I am not referring to questions that indicate that a judge feels one side is stronger than the other; such an indication, indeed, ought to be of assistance to counsel and to the other judges, showing what argument must be met if he is to be argued out of his position. No, I am referring to comments indicating that the judge feels that the case before him is to be decided a certain way because of its genre (civil rights, prisoner, environmental, labor, etc.) or the nature of the party (youth, conscientious objector, militant, alien, etc.) or its magnitude (trivial amount of money, a petty privilege).

Because competent counsel who take the trouble to see how their cases might look to an objective or even a hostile decider can easily predict these reactions, I think it is generally the path of wisdom to challenge the judges to overcome their biases. That is, if a judge comes to argument incensed at the plaintiffs, who he deems a scruffy group of irresponsible youth trying to make trouble in an otherwise peaceful town, counsel would do well to begin, "Your Honors, this case is important just because it looks so trivial. I suspect that none of you would subscribe to the views that the plaintiffs are trying to disseminate in their town. You might deem them immature, shallow, and troublesome without any redeeming merit. That, of course, is exactly how the town authorities felt. And that is precisely why we have a First Amendment, not to permit people to talk about popular ideas – no amendment is needed for *that* – but for just such ideas as those of plaintiffs here." With such a beginning, the wind is out of the judge's sail; counsel has put the case the way the judge sees it – as an irresponsible group merchandising some petty or wrong-headed ideas; all this conceded, however, the legal issue remains and it is an important one.

Just as all judges at times exhibit one or more of the above foibles, so do they reach excellence on occasion, the finest judges reaching it quite often. The profile of the appellate judge at his best would look like this:

> He is well prepared. He has read not only the briefs but the opinion of the judge or agency whose action is being appealed. He has also read a few critical parts of the record – the colloquy between court and counsel when a question was objected to, the entire charge to the jury, a series of intertwining statutes, or the fine print in a construction contract or insurance policy.
>
> He has thought out one or more useful hypothetical questions.
>
> He presses both sides with a few well chosen questions.
>
> He often obtains concessions from counsel that narrow the issues to be decided.
>
> Not infrequently his questioning reveals that there is some issue which exists but which neither side has treated.
>
> At the conclusion of the oral presentation and his colloquies with counsel, all the judges of the panel are likely to see that their own views have changed: the case now appears much more simple than they had thought . . . or much more difficult.

JURY LAWYER
(Without a Jury)

A lawyer who makes the mistake of thinking that three or more appellate judges sitting behind a bench respond to the same approaches as do six to twelve jurors sitting in a jury box.

An effective jury lawyer is deservedly regarded in the public mind as the most formidable kind of advocate the legal system produces. He must be at home with human nature, and use all of his many opportunities – direct examination, cross-examination, objections to evidence, colloquies with the judge, final argument to the jury, and his very presence throughout a trial – to create the confluence of law, facts, and feelings that will move the jury to vote for his client.

In arguing an appeal, the advocate has a very limited time. In that time he is limited to two activities: making a presentation of his own design and answering questions. By this time, there is no longer any freedom to try to develop favorable facts; they have been decided. In the overwhelming majority of cases the only question is the application of law to those facts. This does not mean that "feelings" of the judge play no part. They do. The appellate judges are also human. They care about who is right and who is wrong, who has been harmed, what to do about it. But they, unlike a jury, must be persuaded that the law requires a certain result, notwithstanding feelings to the contrary. So although I have the highest respect for a good jury lawyer, and feel that there is no reason why he cannot make an excellent presentation before an appellate court, I think he must recognize the rather rarified and limited forum he is entering. Merely to rely on his jury skills is not enough. Here, for example, are my notes of one appellate argument by one of the recognized leaders of the criminal defense bar in a large city:

> "He spoke in such a low key and yet with such certainty that somehow, instead of instilling confidence, he made me wonder (having read the government's brief) if he was omitting some key facts . . . and indeed he was. Then for such a veteran to call one of us judges 'Justice' put me off. I gave him extra time to speak to a critical issue that he had not had time to address. He misused it on rhetoric in vacuo."

The weaknesses and strengths of a jury lawyer who is unaccustomed to appearing in an appellate court are suggested in my notes of the appearance of a lawyer from a distant state who claimed that the trial judge had erred in denying his motion for a new trial without holding an evidentiary hearing. We had seriously considered issuing an opinion without holding oral argument but felt that such an eleventh hour decision, on the eve of argument, would be unfair to counsel. Here is how his presentation appeared to me:

> "About 45 years old. Solo, rough and tumble. His opener: 'My client is not arguing to stay out of jail because he is *in* jail.' He has an uphill fight in arguing error in the judge's denying his client a new trial. We so warned him. He is indifferent to our warning. He is obviously a good jury lawyer. He is uncomfortable in being leashed to specific questions. He obviously thinks we should stay put and silent, just like a jury. He is best when he can talk and wave

his arms without hindrance. Despite all this, I find that he gains in credibility. He ends powerfully: 'Who will be hurt by an evidentiary hearing?' I know the legal answer, but I find it hard to say anything but 'No one' from a common sense point of view.

"The prosecutor is pedestrian, but competent in a low-key, persistent way, probably the best way to deal with pyrotechnics.

"The appellant loses – but, considering that we almost denied argument, the lawyer put up a great fight."

LISTENING

A rare quality in an advocate that, when a judge asks him a question, causes him to suspend his own thinking, concentrate on what the judge is saying, and try to see what bothers him.

It is paradoxical that in this media-dominated age creative listening has become almost a lost art. Its restoration in oral presentations would do much to make optimum use of the short time usually allotted counsel.

All too often counsel's motor is running at such a high r.p.m. that during a judge's question he is engaging in double and even triple thinking: "I'll bet he's worried about that hypothetical in my opponent's brief. In that case I'd better show him why that is an entirely different case. I won't give an inch." In fact, the judge has just put a slightly different hypothetical question, where the

obvious answer favors counsel's position. In other words, the judge has just lobbed an easy ball, which he expects the lawyer to handle decisively. But counsel, assuming that the judge is out to trip him up, is mentally all tied up, trying to fathom the various levels of intrigue. The result is a long, involved answer, another more direct question by the judge, and eventually a begrudging "concession" by counsel that the judge's hypothetical question favors his position. By this time five minutes have flown, counsel has missed an easy chance to score, and the judge regrets having tried to be of help. A bit of absorptive listening would have avoided the contretemps.

On a more primitive level, listening has other uses. I am constantly bemused and wonder what goes on in an advocate's mind when a judge asks him to speak a little more loudly. Counsel appears to listen intently. He apologizes. He delivers a sentence registering fully adequate decibels. And then his voice subsides to his previous inaudible monotone.

Of course listening ought to be practiced throughout one's adversary's presentation as well as during one's own. Catching every inaccuracy and concession of opposing counsel can be important. Equally so is the kind of listening that can suggest to an alert advocate that a judge's question is probably best explained by the fact that he is laboring under a misimpression. He may, for example, be overlooking a stipulation of fact that makes his question off the mark.

Finally, there is often a certain subtle discourse taking place among the judges in their questions and comments to counsel. Although counsel should not quickly assume that a judge's remarks reflect his real views, it may be clear by mid-argument that one judge has pretty well dug himself into a position adverse to counsel's. At this point a lawyer who is a gifted listener will have a sense as to whether he should concentrate his remaining fire on the difficult judge or on his more silent and possibly more open colleagues.

Marshalling

The finale and capstone of an effective oral presentation in which the advocate brings together in succinct, highlighted form all of the facts on all of the legal issues, showing what may previously have been hidden or understressed.

A classic occasion for marshalling confronts a prosecutor meeting a challenge that there was insufficient evidence to support a conviction for, e.g., conspiracy. Mere presence of a defendant at or near the scene of the crime is not enough. The prosecutor's job is to identify the several pieces of evidence that show the defendant to have been in on the planning or execution of the scheme. Here is a typical note: "I thought that this [narcotics] case was one where [counsel for appellant] really had a chance with his entrapment defense. (I think I know when he feels he has throwaways.) But the Assistant United States Attorney was deadly, citing to transcript pages to show instance after instance of prior trafficking and predisposition."

Equally effective is the attorney who can present the cumulative effect of arguments. This is the "even if" approach: "Even if there is appellate jurisdiction and even if the objection was preserved below and even if the trial judge erred in his ruling, nevertheless the error was harmless because ________, ________, and ________."

MASTERY OF THE FIELD

The advocate whose knowledge of the relevant law is so broad and deep that he knows how it developed, how the authorities differ and which ones seem sounder and why, and where in the overall legal landscape this case belongs.

Such mastery goes beyond knowing every case in one's brief and in one's adversary's brief – a double duty of no mean significance and violated by more advocates than I care to remember. Sometimes a judge with a particular expertise in a given field will engage counsel in a discussion of the whole field and the current status of scholarly criticism of the leading case on the subject; the give-and-take will be highly sophisticated, electric, and may well suggest that this is the occasion for us to make some new law in what has become a mare's nest of the law.

My favorite instance of such mastery is the argument of a young woman attorney representing the National Labor Relations Board. My notes begin, "Knows her case – persuasive." Then, "Has good answers." Then, "A rare display of mastery of the field. A judge asked her about a case that was in neither brief. She paused, reflected, and said, 'Yes, Your Honor, I've read it several times. I can just picture what you're referring to. It was on the third page in the right hand column. But that was quite a different situation.' And she proceeded to distinguish the case convincingly. Incredibly good."

FREE FLOATING MINE

An advocate who has enough presence, position or connections to attract clients but who lacks the most essential qualifications of one who would charge a fee for his services.

I call this kind of person a "free-floating mine" because the hazard is hidden, subsurface, but can be encountered anywhere. Such a person does not *look* incompetent; indeed, he may give every indication of prospering. He is well accoutered and speaks well, sometimes elegantly. Perhaps the greatest mystery is that such a purported lawyer has absolutely no doubt of his own mastery of his profession. This is the root of the danger: people all too often accept a person on his own estimate of himself.

Here are my nominees for this category:

"A late thirty-ish solo practitioner begins by announcing that this is his first occasion to argue before us . . . and goes on to prove the point. He was incredibly, embarrassingly inept. When asked a question (the question being asked to relieve him of the pain of arguing), he would say, 'It's in my brief.' We finally terminated his presentation, saying we would most certainly read his brief. After appellee, a competent lawyer, had finished, I asked appellant if he wanted rebuttal. He shook his head, looking to an uninitiated eye as if he had cleverly anticipated everything and needed no more time. He proceeded to sit in the courtroom through several subsequent arguments, very good ones. I wondered, watching his complacent expression, whether he knew how incompetent he was. I concluded that he didn't. He is a floating mine, because he *looks* clean and reassuring and apparently *feels* he is competent."

"Appellant argues with alacrity . . . for the first minute. At the end of the second, he is hopeless. He is forced to waive two issues relating to jury instructions, because he had requested none. I felt ashamed to push him; he might concede his whole case. He reads his argument. When the court's questions demolish his points, he continues to read on complacently as if nothing had happened. He is a youngish solo practitioner who should not be allowed to roam free."

"An entirely frivolous argument on entrapment. His cases had been overruled, but he didn't know it – he had not Shepardized them. But he was so impenetrably stupid that when this was pointed out, he acted as if this were a minor criticism, soon to be forgotten, not a lethal wound."

Moot Court Hallmarks

Those slight but discernible signs of an advocate that indicate that his only prior exposure to appellate advocacy has been in the hot-house atmosphere of a law school moot court experience.

In so labelling this category of presentations I have no intention of pooh-poohing law school moot courts. This was one of my chief activities in law school and I know I derived perhaps ninety percent of any facility I had in oral presentation from moot court. But the fact remains that the very process of contriving suitable cases for students to argue tends to produce homogenized situations, all confined pretty much to traditional "argument" scenarios, with no room for factual explanations, policy explorations, efforts to seek reversal of precedents, concentration on affecting the scope of remedy, etc.

In short, moot court without more is likely to produce advocates smelling ever so slightly of the lamp. Two impressions:

> A young woman law student (under the supervision of a member of our bar) argued. "She is articulate but not convincing. 'Sound of words' department. She sounds as if she were repeating a rehearsed moot court exercise. Her facial expressions also seem rehearsed and divert me from concentrating on the argument."
>
> A young man law student. "The student was good, spoke rapidly but gave good answers. He had notes but was flexible. His newness shows in the constant level of perceived stress; everything is equally important. No change of pace."

Myopia

In appellate advocacy the condition in which counsel is placed because he has never taken the trouble to see beyond his nose, i.e., how his case might appear to those further removed from it than he.

Bobbie Burns called on some power to give us the "giftie" to see ourselves "as ithers see us." Any appellate lawyer worthy of his salt should develop within himself such a gift; but even if he is so wedded to his case that he cannot do this, he should seek help from some associate or a lawyer friend.

Failure to correct for nearsightedness leads otherwise diligent and knowledgeable lawyers to make perfect fools of themselves. Here is some grist from my mill:

> Appellant counsel is from a big firm, expert in his field. "When I try to help clarify his argument, at least for myself, he looks at me as if I am stupid. This chills my interest. Another judge takes over and asks a series of complicated but important questions, which succeed in demonstrating that his most effective argument is one which he has no right to raise. It is not even in his brief. He closes lamely, 'Well, that's my argument.'"

> Appellant represents some institutions that claim the federal government owes them money. Counsel paints a picture of the unfairness of the government's position. We say that we are entirely sympathetic but ask him to address the legal problems. For example, are his clients parties to this litigation? We cannot find where they have been so

admitted. The answer: "No, but . . ." It reminded me of the classic escapist question: "Apart from that, Mrs. Lincoln, did you like the play?"

Appellant, although earnest and deserving of our sympathy, didn't make a good analysis of what we suspected was a losing case. Appellee was very smooth. But he pushed his credibility with us by asking double costs when his brief was only one page, containing two unhelpful citations. Yet, my notes read, "When I chided him, he did not seem at all bothered, could not see how we could fault his brief."

Appellant's counsel was endeavoring to show that a letter constituted a threat in violation of a statute. But the real question was whether the letter ever resulted in any harm, loss, or prejudice to the recipient. Counsel obviously had ignored this issue and merely rehearsed the fact of the letter's existence.

"**Judge:** You're simply going through the evidence. But the trial court found no loss or prejudice.

"**Counsel:** Very well, I'll take that advice.

"**Judge:** You needn't.

"**Counsel:** Perhaps I must."

This veneer of indulgent urbanity unsuccessfully masked an obstinate myopia.

In a case involving seizure of a formidable amount of marijuana from a ship, counsel for appellants, who had a number of substantial issues to argue, also claimed that there was no basis for thinking that the quantity of marijuana justified the inference that it was to be used commercially. If we would only assume that each of the dozen people on board consumed x grams a day, every day, for the ten month voyage, the entire quantity would have gone for merely personal use. This, of course, was within the realm of possibility, but one suspects that had counsel made a "dry run" of this argument with other, less involved associates, the argument would not have seen the light of the court-room.

"With wonderful naivete, in light of this client's notorious reputation as the biggest cheat since Ponzi, counsel appealed to our sense of fairness to protect his client's 'good will.' The ensuing laughter throughout the courtroom made me concerned." The maintenance of decorum is important but it requires some cooperation from counsel.

A complex contract case, each side represented by senior partners of big firms. Here are my impressions: "The briefs on both sides were meandering, discursive, and unfocused. They were like ships passing in the night: they seemed to describe two different cases. Oral argument – when one considers that each side is being paid handsomely – was undistinguished. Appellant counsel knew the record very well, but tried to push aside the evidence against him; yet this evidence was the only kind worth looking at, to see if it was enough to support the findings. Appellee counsel did not know the record and was overly general; his efforts to simplify made things too simple, i.e., 'the trial judge so found; he has wide discretion; trust him.'" My notes have a postscript: "Although this had been a long and complex trial, the briefs ominous and the arguments pompous, we all decided that at bottom this should be a very simple affirmance, almost wholly relying on the opinion below. The storm had blown itself out."

Had counsel taken pains to see how their case would appear in court, the arguments of both would have focused on the few critical transcript references to controversial evidence supporting the judgment.

SENSE OF PRIORITY

The quality of an advocate who adapts Darwin to appellate presentations by operating on the principle that the processes of artificial selection govern the survival of one's theses.

The dramatic telescoping of time permitted for oral argument in most appellate courts has highlighted as never before the importance of selectiveness as a critical part of the advocate's arsenal. An "instinct for the jugular" is one very important principle of selection: one should not only concentrate on the most vulnerable part of one's adversary's case but lift to the surface and deal with what a disinterested person would think is the weakest link in one's own case.

First, some impressions of the more common phenomenon, a lack of selectiveness, which blurs and dilutes the offerings of some of the most competent advocates:

> A veteran plaintiff's and civil rights attorney. "Knows and cites much law in his long brief. Articulate to a fault. He has all the equipment except an instinct for where he should spend his time."
>
> A well respected woman trial and appellate lawyer. "Formidable but undiscriminating. Rapid fire, intense, hand motions, high intelligence. *But* some lack of sense of priority, perspective, tone setting, authority. Overcomplicated."
>
> A leader of the criminal bar. "Comes before us for the *n*th time as the 'old familiar.' A judge asks a question (as if merely continuing a conversation that had been going on for years). Counsel gets into a long series of refinements of a point. His case diminishes over time, as he lacks both selectivity and conviction. His argument loses coherence and succinctness."
>
> "An outstanding lawyer in all respects. My only caveat: she argues every issue with equal force. I develop a general sense of skepticism. I realize that one should not be expected to throw away issues, but the very best advocates have the knack of uncorking an extra sense of conviction once in a while, without cheapening the currency of their standard argumentation."

My examples of a lively sense of priority all arise from the presentations of lawyers who were given only five minutes.

Perhaps this draconian limitation was such a powerful lever that we should not be surprised at the emergence of selectiveness. After all, one might think that there would be little opportunity to scatter one's shots in such a brief period. Alas, I can say from lugubrious experience that some advocates can do enough meandering in 300 seconds to rival the Maiandros itself.

> Counsel for one of several appellants in a criminal appeal. "He had only five minutes. But he was an old trial lawyer with a sense of the jugular and zeroed in with a sharp focus on the aspect of the trial that most damaged his client."
>
> In a labor-management case, counsel represented an intervenor union supporting the Labor Board's position. He did not attempt to duplicate the Board's arguments but "used his five minutes to give a realistic picture of the not-so-nice background which tends to be overlooked in the sterile laboratory of the appellate courtroom." Although this sort of presentation can be overdone, a little bit was a healthy antidote against too easily dismissing an employer's violation of the collective bargaining laws as "merely technical," a disposition which initially appealed to some of us.
>
> In a contest between a federal grand jury and a state agency, a young attorney represented a local bar association as an amicus curiae. He devoted his efforts to showing the implications of the possible holdings on the nuts and bolts of law practice. My notes read: "Very earnest; what he said in his five minutes deeply affected our attitudes."

Pro Se

A vestigial survival of the Jacksonian principle that any man can perform any public function; the individual who represents himself and does without professional counsel.

The existence of this species is at once the bane and glory of our judicial system. Bane, because of the disproportionate work for the court necessitated by a usually unorganized and irrelevant presentation. Glory, because such individuals do have access to the appellate level as a matter or right, do receive serious consideration, and occasionally prevail. Both the opposing advocate and the court face unique problems, as these two samplings indicate:

"Plaintiff is a persistent pro se. He looks 'straight' enough, late thirties, dark suit, blue and red striped tie. The appeal is so frivolous that appellee justifiably (I think) asks the court to impose the sanction of counsel fees. His relevant knowledge is so little that he baffles the court. The judges get nowhere in their questioning. This is a case where, I think, we should accept the fact that profitable colloquy is out; it takes two to tango. But my colleagues persist and almost make him look respectable. This false appearance of nonfrivolousness deterred us from imposing fees."

A woman pro se protesting discriminatory action by the university she was attending. "She is so emotional that the argument becomes only a form. We feel we cannot press her without provoking a breakdown or blowup." Counsel for the university, a young man from a big firm. "He, too, has his gloves on, is very cautious, dispassionate. The whole thing is sort of a charade."

RAVELING

The process that even the well-prepared advocate fears most: when in the course of an unhindered and efficient weaving of the fabric of argument a single question leads to an answer that gives the court some difficulty, that leads . . . to the utter entanglement of all the strands of what had been a well-ordered argument.

The moral of this entry into our lexicon is: expect the unexpected. Good preparation will minimize the risk. Also, it is entirely possible that what appears to be a devastating question or observance from the bench will later prove to be off target and irrelevant. If something looms up as a relevant and presently unanswerable question (e.g., why is there diversity jurisdiction?) which has never been focused on by the parties or the trial court, perhaps the only respectable recourse for counsel is to ask for a bit of time in which to check the record or to research the point and file a memorandum.

The following examples are not sensational. They are not intended to portray substandard counsel, but merely to record some instances where I could sense an apparently strong case beginning to ravel. The only criticism I would make is that these counsel for appellees came to court a bit too confident.

Government counsel in a case involving the deportation

of an immigrant treated the case as routine. The issue was whether immigration authorities could arrest an immigrant after a search without probable cause. The authorities on point were few and dubious but counsel made no effort to give us additional references or to defend the few in the brief. As questioning persisted, with the repetition of unenlightening answers, the significance of the case rose in the minds of each judge. Our disposition to affirm in a brief opinion had changed. Indeed, ultimately we reversed.

Counsel for the Commissioner of Internal Revenue "starts smugly and impassively. He has a Tax Court opinion going for him. Then a judge asks a well thought out series of questions that shake him. He finds it impossible to defend the opinion."

A claim by a teacher that a college had improperly discharged him. The college won at trial, and had an impressive brief. But the record made in the court below as to the college's reasons for firing was a skeleton of what it should have been had a series of obvious questions been asked.

The judges' questions focused on the sparseness of the record. What must have looked like an open-and-shut case had turned in a horserace.

An elderly insurance company lawyer was defending a judgment against a young attorney from a small firm. The young attorney had a strong evidentiary point but wasted time in arguing that a jury instruction was reversible error because in addition to the words "clear and convincing," the court should have painted the lily by adding "unequivocal." Unaccountably the insurance lawyer, who had a good, tight case, answered at some length the "unequivocal" argument. Finally, a judge interjected, "Your vigor on this issue is, to me, circumstantial evidence of the substance of your brother's argument." To compound the misstep, the lawyer did not have the transcript reference to rebut appellant's srongest argument. If appellee won this case, it was despite, not because of, the oral presentation. He had done his best to pluck defeat out of the jaws of victory.

In a case involving the discharge of an employee, the young Board attorney "starts out by confidently criticizing the employer for invoking the wrong standard of review. Then, when pressed to say just why a clear violation of law by an employee was harmless, counsel smiled nervously and . . . From then on, it is no longer an easy romp."

A lawyer for a municipality is defending an ordinance, which was found valid by the trial court. "A judge puts a hypothetical question, indicating that he is bothered by the vagueness of the ordinance. He suggested a slightly different ordinance which was obviously vague. The answer isn't at all persuasive. I am beginning to see more problems than I did in chambers . . . and this during *appellee's* presentation. After the argument, my colleague says, 'That fellow from __________ would have done better not to argue."

REPUTATION

An advocate's invisible garment, stitched together in his numerous prior appearances before the court, which proclaims him to be either something of a slicker or a straight shooter.

As this definition makes clear, one's general reputation with the public or even with the practicing bar is not the kind of reputation which amounts to a ponderable asset or liability in making an oral presentation. It is rather, as our discussion of candor has noted, the collective memory of the court of the advocate's prior performances.

Some very accomplished lawyers, whose briefs are models of

prose and whose oral arguments are not only polished but elegant, seem to suffer from a chronic inability to resist cutting a corner here and there by omitting a key fact, misrepresenting a holding, distorting the statement of an issue, or generally brushing real problems under the rug of their more than plausible argument. The result is that judges come to argument prepared to play once again the game of identifying the shell under which the pea is hidden.

At the opposite end of the spectrum are lawyers whose briefs and oral presentations are hardly models of excellence and whose intelligence quotient may not be of the highest rank but who have never been known intentionally to mislead the court and who, indeed, have been known to go out of their way to point out both facts and law adverse to their case. Judges' reactions to such lawyers are often to double check the advocate, not to minimize his argument, but to see if the adverse facts and law are quite as weighty as the advocate feared.

Here are two examples of the value of coming into court with an earned reputation for reliability:

> Counsel is a partner from a large firm. "Comes with reputation, not so much of brilliance, but of integrity and solidity. He exploits this by a measured pace, resonant voice impassively detailing the facts."
>
> Counsel represented an unsuccessful plaintiff in a sex discrimination case and made two arguments which could be called "off the wall." My notes: "These outrageous arguments were accepted by us without harsh cavil because the attorney, a solo practitioner, had done yeoman work as court appointed counsel in many cases – with some notable victories."

SCRIBBLER

An advocate who, while sitting at counsel table listening to his adversary's presentation, furiously covers long sheets of yellow foolscap with emphatic jottings.

This activity, although not so obvious or egregious back bench advocacy as violent headshakings and noddings, is so determined and intense that it, consciously or not, amounts to a kind of advocacy. The attorney is mutely but clearly saying, "See here, Your Honors, how many notes I'm having to make. Lord knows I won't have time to correct all the misimpressions and unsound arguments my opponent is making, but I'm at least jotting them down."

The inevitable let-down comes, however, when counsel rises to his feet and makes but one or two, or no, references to the fiery notes that now shall be embalmed with the file of the case about to be closed. Even more mystifying to the bench is the action of counsel for appellant who, having had his say, writes with frenzy during appellee's argument, then makes perhaps one minor correction or observation in rebuttal.

I do not want to be too harsh in criticizing this activity. If it were not accompanied by silent histrionics, I would say it was merely a way of passing a very dull or a very aggravating fifteen or twenty minutes. This, I confess, is why I am an inveterate note taker, even when there is no foreseeable use of such notes. But there is one thing to guard against if one scribbles: one must not let it interfere with listening.

TORTOISE

The advocate who makes an unimpressive start but plods along and finishes first.

This species is of course to be contrasted to his colleague, the hare. I do not recommend striving for an unimpressive beginning but include this character only to give courage to counsel to continue to labor mightily despite some problems at the beginning. Judges are accustomed to changing their minds. My recorded notes on tortoises are as plodding as the beasts themselves:

> An attorney for a municipality. "My first impression: not very bright, scatters his shots. Later I changed my mind. Handles self well. Humble. Knows facts. Reflects fairness. He was conscious of time and conscientiously touched all issues. The city was well served."
>
> Another city attorney. "Cool, deliberate – *listens*. Defends unsympathetic case agreeably. In his sober, quiet way, grows in my esteem."
>
> An attorney for the federal government. "He is mild." I first noted "looks weak." Then I added, "at first but is very good." This, because I also noted, "knowledgeable . . . came through on every question . . . candid."

TRIBUNE
(Impatient)

The advocate, often but not always young, who, representing people with an excellent cause, has his eye on the goal and not on the ball. He therefore is likely to drop the latter.

I bleed for these attorneys. Their hearts are in the right place. Their road is uphill to begin with. Compensation is likely to be minimal or nonexistent. Nevertheless, these factors do not really excuse such defects of professionalism as failure to adhere to the record, to know basic rules of procedure, to keep the client's interest paramount to any larger "cause," to use practical judgment in selecting issues, to concentrate on realizable goals.

My notes begin with instances of poor judgment in handling issues:

> "Counsel advances an extreme theory of state action, very matter-of-factly, as if this were a routine application of existing law. She radiates no sense of the real world, i.e., recognition of the judges' predictable bias against opening the door to this kind of suit." Her argument might have lost in any event, but would have gone further if she had frankly presented her proposition as novel but a logical and just extrapolation of precedent.
>
> Counsel was a "young academic who wastes time on an issue others have left to their briefs. Because of this, and despite his obvious command of the authorities in the field, he does not command the respect he otherwise would have."
>
> Counsel represents a young demonstrator who had been criminally prosecuted and found guilty of a fairly minor infraction of law. The brief was immense, freighted with over half a dozen alleged constitutional issues, none of them valid. My solitary note: "He is bright but his judgment is off." My point is not that he should have refused his client's appeal, but that he should have seized upon his best issue and not diluted his brief and argument with certain losers.

My second group of notes records counsel who lost track of the ball:

> Counsel represented clients who were trying to prevent a municipality from conveying certain property. After hearing much argument about the law, we inquired about the

nature of the order being appealed from. My notes reveal: "The closing is yet to occur and we learn from city counsel that no one objects to a hearing on a motion – not yet made – for preliminary injunction. We quickly remand for lack of appellate jurisdiction."

A young solo practitioner. "Knows a lot but is not practical. His client has now gotten all she wanted from the government agency, but he brought a class action. Yet he does not accuse the agency of bad or arbitrary conduct, only some technical mistake made in good faith. He is rolling out a pile driver to fasten a staple."

Finally, I record "a thoroughly up to date, articulate lawyer, with dramatically poor judgment. His pettifogging, irritating, excessively burdensome tactics, requests, and lengthy, unproductive examination at hearing clearly incensed the trial judge, known for his patience. Seemingly oblivious to the record of almost contemptuous conduct that he had made, he argued on appeal for a host of due process rights that (a) his client had already received, (b) his client clearly did not merit, or (c) existed only in his mind. A case where any objective advice to the client would have been: 'There's no sense in appealing.' Wait till the client gets a bill of costs from appellee."

Unctuousness

The habit of some advocates, who have a sufficiently low opinion of judges to think that they welcome expressions of extreme servility, deference, and laudation.

In a sense the system may be thought to inculcate unctuousness, with the required threshold formality of "May it please the court." Nobody, however, takes this phrase in its literal meaning, "May what I say tickle your fancies." Everyone, or nearly everyone, assumes that it means, "May what I say be found relevant, sound, and helpful to a decision in accordance with law and – if possible – justice."

Some practitioners, however, have deluded themselves into believing that a simulated fervor of deference is appropriate. It takes various forms: the elaborate correction of minutiae in the brief, which we have noted; assumption of an attitude of intimate familiarity; praising judges for the phrasing of questions; elaborate concessions of points thought to have been made by judges; sycophantic references to opinions of various members of the court ("As Your Honor so well put it in __________ . . .").

I suppose that in a world characterized all too often by incivility, I should overlook a little overemphasis in the opposite direction. But why cannot people in general (not just lawyers) understand that the best expression of respect is that which not only is genuine but which also stems from one who respects himself. Uriah Heep, after all, could not have had much of a regard for himself.

WORDS
(Banal and Bizarre)

The major means by which the advocate conveys his thoughts during oral presentation. Notwithstanding their obvious essentiality to the work of an appellate advocate, they are misused in all sorts of ways, from the prosaic to the strange and wonderful, to the lasting delight of the professional listeners, the judges.

A few of the banal uses most commonly encountered are:

"To be honest with Your Honor" (to signify that most of the time the advocate speaks with forked tongue).

"In all candor" (ditto).

"You know . . ." "O.K." (signifying that the attorney is, after all, part of the great American public).

In commenting on a question from a judge that seemingly favors one's argument: "You hit it right on the head" or "Your Honor has put the matter far more accurately than I have." This is what I call "flowing with the court," i.e., assuming that a judge's questions reflect his final leanings in a case.

A senior partner in a New York firm is the last to argue. Feeling very much at home and exuding a bland mastery of the situation, he begins, "I listened with some interest to my brothers' arguments." "Well," I write to myself irritably, "what are you being paid for if not to do at least that?"

Sometimes the use of slatternly, sluggish, banal words cloaks a euphemistic assault with intent to kill: "There are several items omitted from my brother's account of the case either inadvertently *or for some other reason.*"

My last example is not precisely of the banal; although the words are common enough, the episode is somewhat enchanting: Counsel for appellee is a middle-aged city solicitor, quite obviously the beneficiary and product of the traditional political patronage system. He had filed a brief in which his treatment of each of the four issues was, "The District Court's conclusion on this issue was correct." Period. No argument. No citations to authority. When I called him on this, he said, "Well, Your Honor, this is the first time I have ever written a brief this way but I really felt the district court was correct in everything." I found myself unable to come up with an appropriate reply.

Every judge must have his treasured collection of imaginative and bizarre uses of words, the collectibles remaining, incandescent, on the field of battle after the gladiators have long since departed. Here are a few of mine:

A union attorney is defending the conduct of his client against a suit by a disaffected member: "The union's conduct might not have been rational, but it certainly was not irrational. At most it was a-rational."

Counsel: "I want to underscore some of the difficulties that lie ahead if this doctrine is not circumcised."

In the same case the following charming colloquy took place:

Judge: "Is that case in your brief?"

Counsel: "It might be."

Judge: "Wouldn't it be wonderful if it were? . . . You should be happy to know that it is."

Finally, a slick, seasoned, professional counsel for employers in labor-management cases always fights like a terrier. In this case he was challenged by a young woman attorney for the National Labor Relations Board who presented the little drama as if it were the latest stage hit. Counsel for the employers in reply reached a height of indignant rhetoric not likely to be exceeded: "This is an attempt by the Board to weave a mosaic."

X
The Unknown Quantity

Infinitely varied, the Unknown Quantity furnishes a precise fit with the needs of a particular oral presentation, that the most gifted counsel possesses and uses at the critical moment. An essence that defies further definition. It is the search for X that gives the most serious oral advocates both their spur and their reward.